Built from Broke

Budget Smarter, Invest Wisely, and Build Real Wealth Without a Six-Figure Salary

Darrell L. Keller, Jr.

Built from Broke: Budget Smarter, Invest Wisely, and Build Real Wealth Without a Six-Figure Salary

Published by:

Darrell L. Keller, Jr.

Keller Productions

Printed in the United States of America

Amazon Kindle Direct Publishing

Revised Edition

ISBN: 9798316805518

This book is intended solely for educational and informational purposes. The author is not a licensed financial advisor, tax professional, attorney, or certified public accountant. **The contents of this book should not be considered legal, tax, investment, or financial advice**. Readers should seek the guidance of appropriately qualified professionals before making any financial, legal, or investment decisions.

The strategies, scenarios, and data points included in this book are based on general concepts, public information, and personal experience. They are not intended to represent a one-size-fits-all approach, nor do they account for your specific financial situation, goals, or risk tolerance. You are solely responsible for conducting your own due diligence and consulting with a licensed professional before taking action.

All investment examples provided, including those referencing stocks, mutual funds, ETFs, or real estate, are hypothetical and for illustrative purposes only. Past performance is not a reliable indicator of future performance. **All investments carry inherent risks, including the potential for the loss of capital.** High-return investments typically involve higher levels of risk and may not be appropriate for all investors.

This book also discusses investment options such as Roth IRAs, Traditional IRAs, 401(k) plans, real estate holdings, side hustles, and small business ventures. These discussions are intended to provide a basic understanding and starting point for further research. **They do not constitute a recommendation to invest in any specific vehicle, strategy, or product.** The actual performance of such options depends on a variety of individual and market factors.

The content in this book may reference online platforms, websites, tools, and resources that were active and accurate at the time of writing. The author and publisher do not control the content or availability of external sources and are not responsible for any changes, removals, or inaccuracies that may occur after publication.

Built From Broke was outlined and enhanced with the help of free AI tools like ChatGPT—not as a shortcut, but as a demonstration. The goal was to show exactly how everyday people, especially those who want to write, publish, or build a business on a modest income, can use AI to turn ideas into structured content. You don't need to be a professional writer or have a big budget to get started. With the right prompts and a bit of guidance, tools like ChatGPT can help shape your message, organize your thoughts, and give you the confidence to publish your own work and grow your income in new, creative ways. The experiences, however, are entirely the author's (and tips to save money at home are generously contributed by his wife). They are not AI generated content – they are things we do ourselves to build wealth, not waste it. Your experiences may vary – perhaps you can come up with a few money-saving ideas that you can use instead!

That being said, nothing in this book should be interpreted as a guarantee of earnings, profits, or financial outcomes. Any case studies or anecdotes, including references to third-party individuals or businesses, are provided for educational context only. They do not represent average or guaranteed results and are not intended to suggest that you will achieve similar outcomes.

Neither the author nor the publisher assumes any liability for loss, damage, or disruption caused or alleged to be caused, directly or indirectly, by the information contained in this book. By reading this book, you agree that the author and publisher are not liable for your personal financial decisions, actions, or results, under any circumstances.

This book is provided "as is," without warranties of any kind, either express or implied, including but not limited to warranties of accuracy, completeness, fitness for a particular purpose, or non-infringement.

The use of this book and the reliance on any information contained within is at your own risk.

Contents

We would love to hear from you!

We appreciate you reading *Built from Broke: Building Financial Freedom with a Modest Income*! If you found this book helpful, inspiring, or simply enjoyed this book, would you take a moment to give it a review? Your feedback not only helps others but motivates us to keep bringing you great content!

Here's how you can leave a review:

Scan the QR code below to go directly to the book at the Keller Productions Amazon Store

- Or -

Visit your Amazon Orders page, find this book, and click "Write a Product Review."

Your kind words make a difference!

Thank you for supporting Keller Productions!

Introduction: The Myth of Needing a High Income

Building wealth requires the right mindset, discipline, and strategy.

Too many people assume that building wealth is only for the lucky few—those born into money, working high-paying jobs, or somehow connected to the right circles. But the truth is, you don't need to be rich to start getting ahead. What you really need is a plan, a little discipline, and the willingness to start right where you are. This book leans on the same free tools that are already available to you—things like ChatGPT, YouTube creators who teach real skills, and publishing platforms like Amazon KDP—to show that you don't need a trust fund to build something solid. What you need is to start from where you are, focus on financial discipline, and consistently take small, deliberate steps toward your goal.

It's easy to look at the ultra-wealthy and think they have some magical formula for success. Names like **Bill Gates**, **Oprah Winfrey**, and **Warren Buffett** are often synonymous with massive wealth and success. But behind these names are countless stories of humble beginnings and hard-fought journeys. Bill Gates didn't start with millions; he started with a passion for computers and an idea. Oprah grew up in poverty before becoming a media mogul. Warren Buffett was just an ordinary kid with a love for numbers before his investments began to grow exponentially. These stories remind us that financial freedom is attainable for anyone with the right attitude and strategy—no matter how modest their starting point.

Take, for instance, the iconic rags-to-riches story of **Andrew Carnegie**, one of the wealthiest men in American history. Born into a poor family in Scotland, Carnegie emigrated to the United States with his parents when he was just a boy. He started working as a bobbin boy in a cotton mill for a mere $1.20 a week. But his relentless work ethic, his ability to learn, and his eventual investments in the steel industry allowed him to amass one of the greatest fortunes of his time.

It's important to recognize that, while not everyone will become a billionaire, anyone can build wealth through small, consistent actions. **Built from Broke** is designed to show you how you can start from where you are and take actionable steps, no matter how small, to increase your financial independence.

Starting from Where You Are

The first step to building wealth is **accepting your current financial situation**. Many people make the mistake of comparing their finances to others, especially in today's world of social media where the highlights of others' success are put on display. However, **comparison is the enemy of progress**. The key is to start with what you have, no matter how small, and work toward your goals incrementally.

A powerful example of this is the story of **Dave Ramsey**, a financial expert who went from being broke and bankrupt to a multi-millionaire by following the principles of budgeting, saving, and investing. Ramsey's story is compelling because, like Carnegie, he started from humble beginnings and had to work his way back from the bottom after making financial mistakes. His advice isn't about getting rich quickly; it's about changing your habits and thinking long-term.

Ramsey's "Baby Steps" are a set of practical actions that anyone can take, regardless of income level, to gradually improve their financial situation. These steps are:

1. **Save $1,000 for an emergency fund.**
2. **Pay off all debt (except the mortgage).**
3. **Save 3–6 months of expenses for emergencies.**
4. **Invest 15% of income for retirement.**
5. **Save for college and pay off the mortgage.**
6. **Build wealth and give generously.** These steps are grounded in discipline, and while they may seem small, over time they compound into long-lasting financial security.

But why does this approach work? It works because building wealth is a marathon, not a sprint. It's about focusing on the **small wins**, the daily decisions that, over time, can lead to massive change. That's the foundation of this book: understanding that you don't need to start with millions, but you can absolutely make millions from small, consistent actions.

How This Book Will Help You Build Wealth

In this book, we'll walk through practical steps for building wealth, regardless of your current income. The goal is to show you that, **no matter your financial situation**, wealth is within reach. We'll cover essential principles like:

- **Smart budgeting**: How to track your money and prioritize spending.
- **Saving effectively**: The importance of an emergency fund and saving for future goals.
- **Side hustles and earning more**: Exploring additional income streams that can increase your wealth using free tools already available to you.
- **Investing for beginners**: How to start with small amounts and grow your investments over time.
- **Building credit and paying off debt**: The importance of good credit and strategies for reducing debt.

Each chapter will give you actionable tips, real-life examples, and strategies you can implement today. And the most important part? **Consistency**. The journey to financial freedom is built on making progress, even if it's just a little bit at a time.

The Power of Consistency: Small Steps Lead to Big Results

The **power of consistency** cannot be overstated. Just like building a brick wall one brick at a time, the path to financial freedom is made by consistently taking small, manageable actions. You don't need to radically change your lifestyle overnight. Instead, you need to **set realistic goals** and take manageable steps toward them.

The story of **Chris Gardner**, the man behind the movie *The Pursuit of Happyness*, is a perfect example of how persistence pays off. Gardner was homeless, struggling with an infant son to care for, yet he persevered. He worked tirelessly, took small, calculated steps, and eventually became a millionaire. His story shows that no matter where you start, determination and consistent action can lead to remarkable results.

Likewise, **Ramit Sethi**, a personal finance expert and author of *I Will Teach You to Be Rich*, emphasizes that wealth-building is a journey, not a destination. He encourages readers to start small—saving just $10 a week or investing a small amount—and **build from there**. Over time, the returns on that small investment will add up. The most important thing is to begin, even if it's with a small amount.

The Process Begins Today

This book is your guide to starting your journey toward financial freedom, no matter where you are right now. The principles and strategies inside will help you take control of your finances, start saving, begin investing, and most importantly, believe that you can achieve financial freedom.

Remember, you don't need to be rich to get rich—you just need to start, stay disciplined, and take consistent action. The best time to begin was yesterday. The second-best time is today. This book is here to walk you through the process, step by step. It is meant to be positive and uplifting because you *can* do this. I know because I used the exact same tools I am going to tell you about to do it, too – everything from free AI tools like ChatGPT, online instructional content freely available on YouTube, and using free online market-based platforms to market my projects. I'll even introduce you to some fee-based platforms like eBay and Etsy if you wish to market there, too.

It won't always be quick or easy - and you will ALWAYS have critics, review bombers, and unsupportive friends, family, and co-workers who will try to bring you down for whatever reason. This isn't about them; it is about *you* and every smart decision you make brings you closer to financial freedom. You don't need perfection—you just need to start. You *can* do this – **and it starts the very moment you make the decision to begin!**

Chapter 1: The Wealth Mindset

Shifting from Scarcity to Abundance

The first step to building wealth doesn't involve budgets, savings accounts, or investments—it involves your mindset. The way you think about money, wealth, and your financial future has a direct impact on how you manage and grow your finances. For many, the idea of becoming wealthy feels out of reach because they operate from a mindset of **scarcity**. They believe that there's only so much money to go around and that no matter how hard they work, they will always be stuck in their current financial situation.

A scarcity mindset is often rooted in fear—fear of not having enough, fear of not being able to afford things, and fear of failure. If you constantly worry about money, you're not focused on the opportunities available to you. **A scarcity mindset keeps you stuck in survival mode**, reacting to life's challenges rather than proactively creating wealth.

On the other hand, a mindset of **abundance** is about understanding that there are always opportunities to grow, invest, and build wealth—no matter how small your starting point is. People with an abundance mindset don't see wealth as a limited resource; they see it as something that can be created, shared, and multiplied through hard work, discipline, and creativity.

When you adopt an abundance mindset, you open yourself up to new possibilities. You start looking at money as a tool to help you achieve your goals rather than something that is constantly slipping away. This shift in perspective is critical because it will change how you approach every financial decision—from saving to investing and beyond.

Developing Patience and Discipline

Building wealth on a modest income is not an overnight process. It's easy to get discouraged when you don't see instant results, but the key to long-term success is **patience**. Wealth is built over time through consistent actions, and it requires the discipline to stick to those actions, even when progress seems slow.

Look at **Warren Buffett**, one of the wealthiest individuals in the world. Buffett's wealth didn't come from trying to find a quick shortcut or an "easy" way to make money. Instead, he built his fortune by making smart, patient investments over the course of decades. One of his most famous quotes is, "The stock market is a device for transferring money from the impatient to the patient." Patience and discipline are the core principles of Buffett's wealth-building strategy.

The same holds true for you. Wealth doesn't happen overnight, and there will be moments where the progress seems slow. But with patience and consistent action, you'll see the compound effect of your efforts over time. Discipline is key—it's about doing what you know needs to be done, even when it's tough, even when you're tempted to splurge or abandon your savings plan.

The Role of Persistence in Building Wealth

Persistence is often the defining characteristic of those who succeed in building wealth, especially when starting from humble beginnings. If you look at **Andrew Carnegie**, you see a perfect example of persistence. Carnegie didn't come from money. His early years were marked by hard labor and long hours working in factories, yet he never gave up. He continued to educate himself, worked tirelessly, and invested in opportunities that others overlooked.

Persistence doesn't mean working endlessly without seeing results; it means committing to your financial goals even when things don't go as planned. Building wealth is a journey, and like any long journey, there will be setbacks along the way. Whether it's an unexpected medical bill, a car repair, or a dip in the stock market, the important thing is to keep moving forward, even if that means making small adjustments along the way.

Many people give up too soon because they believe that one setback means they can't succeed. But it's the ones who keep going—who adjust, adapt, and keep their eyes on the long-term goal—who ultimately reach financial freedom.

Understanding the Power of Small, Consistent Actions

One of the most important lessons in building wealth is understanding the power of **small, consistent actions**. It's easy to look at others and think that they got rich overnight. But for most people, wealth is built through decades of smart, intentional choices. Small actions—like setting aside $50 for savings every month or investing in a low-cost index fund—might not seem like much at first, but over time, they compound and create significant results.

Think about the story of **The Compound Effect**, a concept introduced by Darren Hardy. The idea is that small, everyday choices—good or bad—add up over time to create big results. Imagine two people: one invests $100 each month, and the other spends that same $100 on impulse buys. After a few years, the person who invested that money will see significant growth, thanks to compound interest.

Building wealth is about focusing on the long-term effects of your small actions. It's not about making drastic changes all at once; it's about setting yourself up for gradual, consistent growth. If you commit to saving and investing a small percentage of your income every month, you'll be surprised at how quickly it adds up over time.

Rethinking Your Relationship with Money

Most people's relationship with money is shaped by fear, insecurity, or a lack of education. But to build wealth, you need to change that relationship. **Money is a tool.** It is not something to be feared, hoarded, or spent recklessly. Money can be used to fund your dreams, provide security, and create opportunities.

Start by understanding that you control your financial destiny. Money isn't something that happens to you—it's something you can manage and grow. It starts with setting clear financial goals. What do you want your life to look like five, ten, or twenty years from now? What will it take to get there? By setting specific financial goals and breaking them down into manageable steps, you take control of your finances and start moving toward the future you desire.

The Importance of Setting Clear Goals

Before you start building wealth, you need to know what you're working toward. **Financial goals give you a clear direction** and help you stay motivated when the going gets tough. Setting goals also allows you to break down your wealth-building journey into manageable, actionable steps.

Let's look at a simple example: If you want to save $10,000 over the next year, that's a big goal. But if you break it down into monthly and weekly targets, it becomes more achievable. You'll know exactly how much you need to save each month and can make a plan for how to achieve it. Whether your goals are short-term (saving for a vacation) or long-term (building a retirement fund), setting clear goals will keep you focused and give you the drive to keep going.

Your goals should be **specific, measurable, and realistic**. For example, instead of saying, "I want to be rich," you could say, "I want to save $500 every month for the next year" or "I want to invest 15% of my income in a diversified portfolio." By setting clear goals, you have a roadmap for success.

Conclusion

Building wealth starts with how you think. If you believe money is always out of reach, it probably will be. But if you start seeing every dollar as a tool—something you can direct and control—you'll begin to realize how much power you actually have. **Developing patience, persistence, and consistency is critical**, as is understanding the power of small, everyday actions. The small choices you make every day matter more than you think. Setting clear goals and deciding to take charge of your finances is what puts you on the path toward real financial freedom.

In the next few chapters, we're going to get into the nuts and bolts—how to budget, save, invest, and grow. But remember: **it all starts here**. None of that works without the right mindset. So, if you're ready to stop drifting and start building, you're exactly where you need to be.

Chapter 2: Smart Budgeting and Money Management

Why Budgeting Matters

When it comes to building wealth, **budgeting** is the cornerstone. Without a clear understanding of where your money is going, it's impossible to take control of your financial situation. A budget gives you a roadmap—it shows you how much money you have, where it's being spent, and where you can make adjustments to free up money for savings, investing, or debt reduction.

Many people avoid budgeting because they feel like it's restrictive or too complicated. They think, "I don't make enough to even budget" or "Budgeting is only for people with lots of money." But budgeting isn't about restricting your spending; it's about **giving every dollar a purpose** so you can manage your money wisely. The truth is, budgeting is even more important when you have a modest income. It ensures that you're living within your means and allocating your resources toward your most important financial goals.

If you're not budgeting, you're essentially letting your money control you instead of taking control of your money. The goal of budgeting isn't to create a restrictive, joyless lifestyle—it's to empower you to spend with intention, save with purpose, and invest with confidence. Why do you need a budget?

One simple formula: Income - Expenses = Surplus (or, if you aren't careful, Deficit).

The 50/30/20 Rule: A Simple Approach to Budgeting

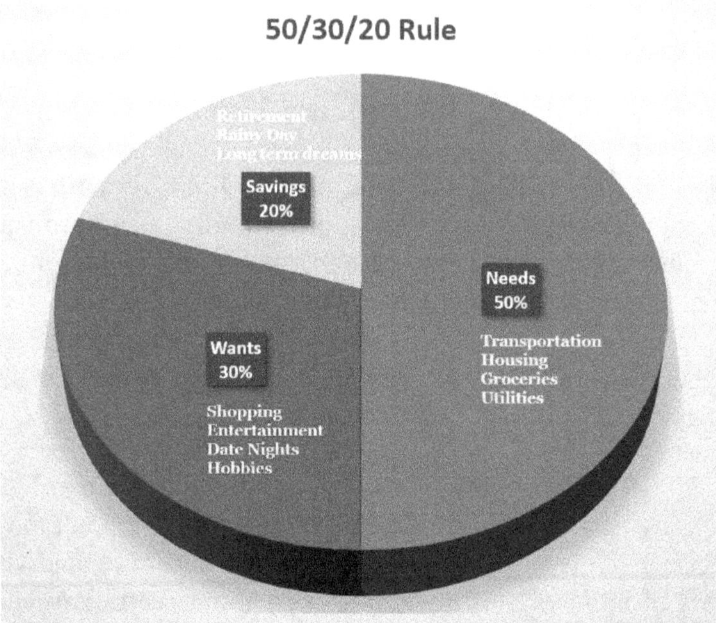

There are many ways to budget, but one of the most straightforward approaches is the **50/30/20 rule**. This rule breaks down your income into three categories:

- **50% for Needs:** These are expenses you must pay to live—things like rent or mortgage, utilities, food, insurance, and transportation.

- **30% for Wants:** This includes discretionary spending like entertainment, dining out, shopping, and vacations.

- **20% for Savings and Debt Repayment:** This portion should be allocated toward building your emergency fund, paying off debt, and investing for your future.

The **50/30/20 rule is simple**, but it can be life-changing. If you start by tracking how much you spend in each of these categories, you'll get a clearer picture of where your money is going. For many people, this is an eye-opening experience. They often find that they're spending more on wants than they realized, and cutting back on those "non-essential" expenses will free up money to save and invest.

It's important to note that this is just a guideline. If you have a lot of debt or are struggling to make ends meet, your savings rate might be lower at first. On the other hand, if you have a steady income and no debt, you might be able to allocate a higher percentage to savings and investments.

Tracking Your Expenses: A Necessary Step for Financial Control

The first step in budgeting is **tracking your expenses**. Before you can allocate money to savings or investments, you need to know where your money is going. For a full month, track every dollar you spend—every cup of coffee, every meal out, every subscription. Write it down or use an app to monitor your spending.

Tracking your expenses might feel tedious at first, but it's essential. Many people are shocked by how much they spend without realizing it. Small, daily purchases can add up quickly. **That daily $5 coffee? It's $150 a month.** Dining out for lunch every day? That's over $200 a month. Tracking these expenses will help you see where you can cut back and reallocate that money to more important areas—like paying down debt or saving for future goals.

Once you've tracked your expenses for a month, categorize them:

- **Fixed Expenses**: These are the regular bills that stay the same each month, like rent or mortgage, utilities, and insurance.
- **Variable Expenses**: These are expenses that change from month to month, like groceries, gas, and entertainment.
- **Discretionary Expenses**: These are non-essential items, like subscriptions, eating out, and luxury items.

By separating your expenses into categories, you can get a clearer picture of where to make adjustments. If your goal is to save more money, start by cutting back on discretionary expenses. If you're serious about building wealth, this is one of the easiest ways to free up more money for savings and investing.

Cutting Back on Expenses Without Sacrificing Quality of Life

Now that you have a clear picture of your spending, it's time to make adjustments. But cutting expenses doesn't mean sacrificing your quality of life or giving up the things you enjoy. It's about being intentional with your spending.

Let's say you're spending $200 a month on dining out. **Instead of cutting it out completely, challenge yourself to reduce it to $100.** That's still a significant amount of dining out, but it allows you to free up $100 that you can put toward savings or debt reduction. You don't have to be extreme, but you do need to be intentional. The goal is to find the balance between enjoying your life and ensuring that you're saving and investing enough for your future.

Here are a few tips for cutting back without sacrificing your lifestyle:

- **Meal planning and cooking at home**: Instead of dining out, plan your meals for the week and cook at home. Not only will this save you money, but it will also improve your health.
- **Cancel unused subscriptions**: Take a look at your recurring subscriptions (magazines, streaming services, gym memberships) and cancel the ones you don't use.
- **Buy in bulk**: For essentials like toiletries, canned goods, or cleaning supplies, buying in bulk can save you money in the long run.
- **Shop smarter**: Look for sales, use coupons, and take advantage of discount stores to buy what you need at a lower price.

Small adjustments like these can make a big difference. It's not about being frugal—it's about **making smart choices** that align with your financial goals.

Setting Financial Goals and Prioritizing Your Spending

Once you've created a budget and started tracking your expenses, it's time to set financial goals. Financial goals give you something to work toward and help you prioritize your spending. Without clear goals, it's easy to get side-tracked or discouraged when you're not seeing immediate results.

Start by setting both short-term and long-term goals. Short-term goals might include things like building an emergency fund or paying off credit card debt. Long-term goals could be saving for retirement, buying a home, or building an investment portfolio.

Once your goals are in place, use them to guide your spending decisions. If your goal is to save for an emergency fund, make that a priority in your budget. If you want to pay off high-interest debt, allocate a larger portion of your income to paying down those balances. The clearer your goals, the easier it will be to stay motivated and make progress.

Emergency Funds: The First Step to Financial Security

Before you start investing or making big purchases, the first thing you need to do is **build an emergency fund**. Life happens—unexpected medical bills, car repairs, or job loss can all throw off your financial plan. An emergency fund provides a cushion, so you don't have to rely on credit cards or loans when the unexpected happens.

The general rule of thumb is to have 3-6 months' worth of living expenses in an emergency fund. If you're just starting out, aim for at least $1,000. It might take time to build this up, but even small contributions can make a difference. Start by saving just $50 or $100 per month until you have a safety net in place.

Using Technology to Simplify Budgeting

In today's world, there are many tools and apps that can make budgeting easier. Whether you prefer to track your expenses on paper or through a digital tool, the key is consistency. Apps like **Credit Karma**, **YNAB (You Need a Budget)**, and **EveryDollar** can help you track your income and expenses automatically, making budgeting less time-consuming and more accurate.

These apps allow you to set spending limits, track your financial goals, and receive notifications when you're nearing your budget limits. They can also help you analyze your spending habits and find areas for improvement.

Conclusion

Budgeting is the foundation of wealth-building. Whether you're starting with a modest income or have a bit more flexibility, a budget allows you to track your expenses, prioritize your spending, and allocate funds for savings and investments. The goal is to take control of your money, make intentional decisions, and stay committed to your long-term financial goals.

In the next chapter, it's time to shift focus from saving to earning. The next chapter is all about growing your income strategically—not through random hustle, but with intention. We'll look at how building the right combination of skills (often called skill stacking), leveraging your network, and launching side hustles can open doors to new income streams. Whether you're looking to move up in your career, pivot to something new, or simply add a cushion to your budget, these strategies will help you grow your income in ways that align with your strengths and long-term goals.

Chapter 3: Growing Your Income Strategically

Growing your income is a critical piece of the wealth-building puzzle. While budgeting and saving lay the groundwork, income growth is the fuel that accelerates your financial journey. This chapter will explore the strategic steps you can take to increase your earnings, even if you're starting from a modest base. The focus will be on practical, actionable strategies that regular people can implement—no inheritance, lottery win, or Silicon Valley startup required.

Understanding Your Current Value

Before you can grow your income, you need to understand what you currently offer in the marketplace. This starts with an honest assessment of your skills, experience, and the demand for what you do. You must know your value to negotiate higher wages, seek promotions, or explore other career paths. One effective method is to research the average salary for your position in your area using online tools like Glassdoor, Payscale, or the Bureau of Labor Statistics. This gives you a benchmark to evaluate whether you're being compensated fairly.

Self-assessment tools can also help you identify transferable skills that are valuable in other roles or industries. For example, if you have strong communication and organizational skills, these may open doors to management or administrative positions even if your background isn't directly in those fields.

Skill Stacking and Lifelong Learning

To grow your income, you must become more valuable. This doesn't necessarily mean going back to college for an expensive degree. Many high-income individuals build wealth through "skill stacking"—combining multiple competencies that are individually common but rare in combination.

For instance, being proficient in graphic design isn't rare. Knowing how to market a product isn't rare. But if you can design compelling visuals *and* market them effectively online, you're suddenly positioned for freelance work, entrepreneurship, or higher-paying jobs.

Online platforms like Coursera, Udemy, and LinkedIn Learning make it easier than ever to learn new skills. Investing just a few hours a week into learning technical skills (coding, digital marketing, financial planning) or soft skills (leadership, negotiation, public speaking) can pay off substantially over time.

Certification and Training Programs

Many well-paying jobs require certifications that take far less time and money than traditional degrees. Electricians, HVAC technicians, project managers (PMP), Google-certified IT professionals, and certified medical coders are all examples of roles where certification programs can boost your income.

Even within white-collar professions, certifications often carry weight. A Six Sigma certification in quality management, for instance, can help you stand out in manufacturing or logistics sectors. Becoming a certified Scrum Master can lead to opportunities in project management or software development.

Choose certifications that align with your interests and the market demand in your area. A few thousand dollars and a few months of study can open the door to much higher earning potential.

The Power of Networking

People often underestimate the role of networking in income growth. Many of the best job opportunities never get posted publicly. They come through word-of-mouth or direct referrals. Building a strong professional network increases your chances of learning about—and landing—those opportunities.

Networking doesn't mean handing out business cards at events. It means forming genuine relationships, helping others, and staying active in your professional community. This can be done through LinkedIn, industry-specific forums, local business meetups, or volunteering.

Having a mentor can also be a game-changer. Someone further along in your desired career path can offer insights, guidance, and sometimes even direct job referrals. Never hesitate to ask someone you respect for a quick coffee chat or informational interview.

Side Hustles with High Potential

Sometimes, the best way to grow your income is to add an entirely new stream. Side hustles can start small and scale over time into substantial sources of income—or even replace your full-time job.

Look for side hustles that match your skills and interests. Freelancing in writing, editing, or graphic design is a great fit for creatives. Rideshare driving, food delivery, or remote customer service are flexible options for those with reliable transportation.

One particularly powerful side hustle is **Amazon Kindle Direct Publishing (KDP)**. This platform allows anyone to publish books—without upfront printing costs—and earn royalties for each copy sold. You can publish low-content books like journals, planners, or coloring books, or you can write full-length nonfiction or fiction titles.

This book was built with the help of AI—but not in the way people sometimes assume. The ideas, experiences, and stories are all real. What AI helped with was the heavy lifting that often holds writers back: outlining chapters, drafting transitions, organizing thoughts, and keeping everything on track. Tools like ChatGPT made the process faster and more manageable, especially when time and resources were limited. For people who want to publish a book but aren't sure how to start – especially if writing isn't their strong suit – AI offers a way forward. That's exactly how *Built From Broke* came together. The tech didn't write the story. It helped make the story possible. It can make yours possible, too.

To get started with Amazon KDP:

1. Create a free account on kdp.amazon.com.

2. Decide what kind of book you want to publish. Low-content books are ideal for beginners. These include notebooks, gratitude journals, and undated planners.

3. Use free tools like Canva or Book Bolt to design your cover and interior. Amazon has templates to help you format everything correctly.

4. Upload your book, add a title and description, and choose keywords and categories for discoverability.

5. Set your price and hit publish. Amazon handles the printing, shipping, and payment processing. You earn royalties for every sale.

Many people have successfully built passive income streams this way. One popular teacher is **Sean Dollwet**, who shares free tutorials on YouTube explaining how to publish on KDP, create high-quality low-content books, and optimize for search visibility. His channel is a great resource for beginners who want to learn step-by-step and avoid common pitfalls. He covers niche research, keyword strategy, cover design, and marketing in simple, easy-to-follow videos. It was Sean Dollwet who taught me how to do it, too. Indeed, his work helped make this very book possible. The best part? Once your book is live, it can generate sales indefinitely.

Free tools like ChatGPT, along with creators who generously share their knowledge are making it possible for everyday people to build real, lasting income without needing a big budget or a business degree. For those who don't have thousands to invest, these resources can be the difference between staying stuck and finally getting started. Whether it's outlining a book, setting up a product listing, or learning how to publish on Amazon KDP, the information is out there—and it's free. What used to take a team of experts and a lot of money can now be done with a laptop, an idea, and a little bit of time.

That's the real power of tools like this: they level the playing field and give regular people a shot at creating something permanent. Something that works for them—even while they sleep. As you step into the world of AI-assisted content creation, know this: not everyone will be on board. Some people flat-out dislike anything they think might be AI-generated, and a few will go out of their way to criticize or "expose" it. That's okay. It comes with the territory. Every new tool that makes life easier or more accessible has faced resistance—from automobiles to personal computers and the internet to self-publishing. What matters most is the value you're providing and the impact you're trying to make. If you're using the tools available to you, being honest about your process, and putting real effort into your work, then you have every right to create, publish, and grow—no matter what anyone else thinks. Your experiences are your own and no critic can take that from you, even if AI helps you bring those experiences to others.

Negotiating a Raise or Promotion

If you're employed, one of the most direct ways to increase your income is by negotiating a raise. But you can't just walk into your boss's office and ask for more money without preparation.

Start by documenting your achievements, measurable contributions, and how you've helped your team or company succeed. Have specific examples ready—"I improved process X, which saved the company Y dollars over Z months." Timing is also important. Annual review periods, after completing a major project, or following a positive performance evaluation are ideal times to make your case.

If your company can't offer a raise due to budget constraints, consider negotiating for other benefits like additional vacation days, a better title, or opportunities for professional development—all of which can enhance your long-term earning potential.

Switching Employers Strategically

Staying with one company for too long can sometimes limit your income growth. While loyalty has its place, data shows that employees who switch jobs every 2–3 years tend to see faster wage increases.

Job hopping doesn't mean being unreliable—it means being strategic. Make sure you leave roles on good terms, with references lined up and no burned bridges. Use each job to build new skills and expand your professional network. Look for companies with a track record of promoting from within, offering professional development, and paying at or above market rates. These companies are more likely to support your income growth long term.

Starting a Microbusiness

For many people, starting a small, home-based business is a practical path to wealth. Microbusinesses don't require massive startup capital or complicated infrastructure. With the right niche and a bit of hustle, you can grow your income significantly.

A microbusiness typically involves one person or a very small team, often operating out of a home office, garage, or online platform. These businesses are lean, flexible, and focused on delivering value in a niche area. Here are some examples, along with how to get started with each:

1. Virtual Assistant Services

What It Is: Providing remote administrative, scheduling, email, or customer service support to businesses.

How to Start:

- Choose your services: calendar management, data entry, social media management, etc.
- Create a profile on platforms like Upwork, Fiverr, or Freelancer.
- Consider a short course from websites like Skillshare or Udemy to learn skills and become competitive.

Tools Needed: Zoom, Calendly, Asana or Trello.

2. Print-on-Demand Merchandise

What It Is: Designing graphics for T-shirts, mugs, posters, tote bags, and more, which are printed and shipped by a third-party provider only when a sale is made.

How to Start:

- Set up free accounts on platforms like Printful, Printify, or TeeSpring. The connect your account to Etsy or Shopify for selling.
- Use Canva or Adobe Express to design merchandise.
- Promote products on social media and targeted ads.

Low Overhead: You don't pay for inventory or shipping, which keeps startup costs low.

3. Freelance Bookkeeping

What It Is: Providing bookkeeping and financial record-keeping for small businesses, freelancers, or non-profits.

How to Start:

- Take a certification course in QuickBooks or Xero (many are online and affordable).
- Create a LinkedIn profile focused on bookkeeping services.
- Offer services on websites like Upwork, Freelancer, or directly to local small businesses.
- Join the American Institute of Professional Bookkeepers for networking and credibility.

Pro Tip: Start by offering monthly services at a flat rate. Most small businesses want consistency and simplicity.

4. Tutoring or Online Coaching

What It Is: Teaching a subject you're skilled in (math, writing, SAT prep, music) or offering coaching (fitness, career, mindset, productivity).

How to Start:

- Use platforms like Wyzant, Tutor.com, or Teachable to find students or sell online courses.
- Offer free sessions on social media or in local Facebook groups to build credibility.

- Develop lesson plans and offer personalized services to justify higher pricing.
- Create a scheduling system using Calendly or Acuity.

Scalability: You can grow this into group classes or digital courses for passive income.

5. Pet Sitting or Dog Walking

What It Is: Providing care, attention, and exercise to pets while their owners are away.

How to Start:

- Register on platforms like Rover, Wag!, or Care.com.
- Get bonded and insured to build trust.
- Market your services in local Facebook groups and with flyers in community centers or vet clinics.
- Offer package deals (e.g., weekly walking plans) for recurring income.

Great For: People who love animals and want a physical, outdoor job.

How to Choose the Right Microbusiness for You

- **Align with your skills and interests.** If you hate spreadsheets, bookkeeping won't be sustainable. But if you love helping others, tutoring or coaching could be perfect.

- **Test demand before committing.** Offer services to friends, family, or local community members. Validate the idea before going all in.
- **Start lean.** Use free or low-cost tools. Avoid taking on debt.
- **Track everything.** Keep records of income, expenses, clients, and feedback. This helps when scaling or reporting income for taxes.

Getting Started: Step-by-Step Plan

1. **Identify a skill or service you can offer.** Think about what people already ask you for help with.
2. **Research the market.** Is there a need for this service locally or online?
3. **Choose a platform.** Etsy, Upwork, Fiverr, Facebook Marketplace, or your own website.
4. **Create a brand.** A name, logo (use Canva), and basic visual identity help you stand out.
5. **Launch soft.** Start with friends and family or offer a discount for first-time customers to build testimonials.
6. **Market regularly.** Social media, email newsletters, and community networking are key.
7. **Reinvest profits.** Buy better tools, run ads, or outsource repetitive tasks.

A successful microbusiness may not make you rich overnight—but it can become a powerful source of consistent income. Many entrepreneurs started with small ideas like these and went on to build six-figure or seven-figure enterprises. When you take control of your time and recognize the value you bring to the table, you open the door to new ways of earning. Paired with smart money habits and a long-term approach to investing—which we'll cover next—your small business or side hustle can become a powerful part of how you build lasting wealth.

Conclusion

Income growth is about being proactive. You must actively look for ways to add value—to your employer, your clients, or the market at large. Whether through skill-building, side hustles, negotiation, or entrepreneurship, you have more control over your earning potential than you might think.

This chapter has provided a roadmap. It's up to you to take the next step. In the following chapter, we'll explore how to make your money work for you through investing, so that increased income becomes increased wealth, not just increased spending. We'll break down smart investment strategies that are accessible, practical, and proven. You'll learn the power of dollar cost averaging, the long-term benefits of contributing to retirement accounts like 401(k)s and IRAs, and how real estate can play a role in building wealth. We'll also cover one of the most overlooked investments—yourself. From education to health to personal development, investing in your own growth often yields the greatest return. This chapter is about building a foundation that works for you now and pays off for decades to come.

Chapter 4: Building Wealth Through Smart Investments

One of the most powerful tools for creating long-term wealth is investing. While earning more and managing your budget lays the groundwork, true financial independence often comes from making your money work for you. This chapter will explain the basics of investing, eliminate common myths, and give you the tools you need to get started even if you don't have a large income.

As we work through this chapter, I will tell you what worked for me. Your results WILL vary because the markets change literally every day. I am in no way giving investment advice, nor should you take anything in this book as investment advice. **You must invest at your own risk and you may lose money with any investment you make. I am not responsible for any losses or gains you make in the market, though I do wish you the best of good fortune!**

Understanding the Power of Compound Interest

Albert Einstein is often credited with calling compound interest the eighth wonder of the world. Whether or not he actually said it, the sentiment remains true: compound interest is one of the greatest wealth-building tools available.

Example: If you invest $200 a month at an average return of 8%, in 30 years you'll have over $280,000. But here's the kicker—you will have only invested $72,000 of your own money. The rest is growth on growth.

The earlier you start investing, the more powerful compound interest becomes. Time is the most important factor. You don't need to be rich to begin—**you just need to be consistent**.

Stocks: The Cornerstone of Long-Term Investing

When people think of investing, the stock market is usually the first thing that comes to mind. While it has its risks, over long periods the stock market has consistently delivered average annual returns of 7-10%.

Types of Stock Investments:

- **Individual Stocks:** Buying shares of a single company like Apple, Amazon, or Tesla. Riskier, but potentially high reward.

- **Index Funds:** These are baskets of stocks that track a market index like the S&P 500. Lower risk and great for beginners.

- **ETFs (Exchange-Traded Funds):** Similar to index funds, but trade like stocks. Great for low fees and diversification.

Where to Start:

- Open a brokerage account on platforms like Fidelity, Vanguard, or Charles Schwab.

- If you're brand new, consider using beginner-friendly apps like Robinhood or M1 Finance.
- Set up automatic contributions to invest monthly.

Dollar-Cost Averaging

This is a strategy where you invest a fixed amount of money at regular intervals, regardless of the market's condition. It reduces the risk of investing a large sum at the wrong time and ensures you stay disciplined.

Why It Works: You buy more shares when prices are low and fewer when prices are high, averaging out your cost over time.

Retirement Accounts: Tax-Advantaged Investing

If you're not using retirement accounts, you're likely leaving money on the table. These accounts give you tax breaks that supercharge your wealth-building. Let's break down the three major types of retirement accounts and when each makes the most sense.

401(k): The Employer-Sponsored Workhorse

A 401(k) is a retirement plan offered by many employers. It allows you to contribute pre-tax income (meaning your taxable income is lowered in the year you contribute), and your investments grow tax-deferred until retirement.

- **Employer Match:** Many employers match your contributions up to a certain percentage. If your employer offers a match, always contribute enough to get the full match—this is essentially free money.

- **Contribution Limit (2025):** $23,000 per year if you're under 50; $30,500 if you're 50 or older.
- **When to Choose:** If you have access to an employer match, start here. It's the fastest way to boost your retirement savings.
- **Risks:** You may have limited investment options based on what your employer offers. Fees can also vary.

Roth IRA: Tax-Free Growth for the Long Haul

A Roth IRA allows you to contribute after-tax income. Your investments grow tax-free, and you can withdraw the money in retirement without paying any taxes on the gains.

- **Contribution Limit (2025):** $7,000 per year if you're under 50; $8,000 if you're 50 or older.
- **Income Limits:** Eligibility phases out at higher income levels (check current IRS guidelines).
- **When to Choose:** If you're young, in a lower tax bracket, or expect to be in a higher tax bracket during retirement, a Roth IRA is ideal.
- **Risks:** Contributions are made with after-tax dollars, so there's no immediate tax benefit. However, long-term tax-free growth is often worth it.

Example: A 25-year-old contributes $6,000 a year to a Roth IRA, invested in a broad stock market index fund earning 8%. By age 60, they'll have over $1 million—and every dollar can be withdrawn tax-free.

Traditional IRA: Flexible Tax Breaks

A Traditional IRA allows for pre-tax contributions (if you meet certain income requirements), which can lower your current taxable income.

- **Contribution Limit (2025):** Same as Roth IRA.
- **When to Choose:** If you don't have access to a 401(k) and want a tax deduction now, or if your income is too high for a Roth IRA.
- **Risks:** You'll pay taxes on withdrawals in retirement, and early withdrawals before age 59½ come with penalties.

Which One Is Right for You?

Here's a simple way to think about it:

- **Start with your 401(k) if your employer offers a match.** It's free money, and the compounding starts immediately.
- **Next, consider a Roth IRA** if you're young or in a lower tax bracket. You'll lock in tax-free growth.
- **If your income is too high for a Roth, or you need a tax deduction now, go with a Traditional IRA.**

If you're self-employed or have a side hustle, you can also open a **Solo 401(k)** or a **SEP IRA**, which allow you to contribute much more annually and are tax-advantaged as well.

Where to Get Started:

- **Vanguard, Fidelity, or Charles Schwab** are great places to open IRAs. Their fees are low, and they offer a wide range of index funds.
- Use robo-advisors like **Betterment or Wealthfront** if you want automation and hands-off investing.
- Apps like **Acorns** and **SoFi** offer IRA options with simplified interfaces for beginners.

Real Estate: Tangible and Profitable

Real estate has long been a proven path to wealth. From cash flow to tax benefits, real estate offers unique advantages not found in stocks or bonds. And despite what many believe, you don't need to be wealthy to get started.

Entry-Level Strategies:

1. **House Hacking:**
    - Buy a multi-unit property (duplex, triplex, fourplex), live in one unit, and rent out the others. Your tenants help pay your mortgage.
    - Even if you buy a single-family home, you can rent out extra bedrooms. Platforms like Facebook Marketplace and Craigslist make finding tenants easy.

- Use FHA loans to buy with as little as 3.5% down if it's your primary residence.
- Example: Buy a duplex for $200,000. With an FHA loan, you might only need $7,000 down. Rent out one unit for $1,000/month and live in the other. Your cost of living drops dramatically, and you're building equity every month.

2. **REITs (Real Estate Investment Trusts):**
    - Publicly traded REITs allow you to invest in real estate without owning property. You can buy shares just like a stock.
    - Great for beginners or those who don't want to deal with property management.
    - Start with as little as $50 on platforms like Fundrise, RealtyMogul, or buy REIT ETFs through Vanguard or Fidelity.
3. **Turnkey Rentals:**
    - These are properties that are renovated and already have tenants. Companies sell these as "ready to go" investments.
    - Websites like Roofstock, Norada Real Estate, and HomeUnion help investors buy cash-flowing properties in affordable markets.
    - Ideal if you live in an expensive city but want to invest in affordable areas.

4. **Short-Term Rentals (Airbnb):**
    - Turn a room or an entire property into a vacation rental.
    - You can start small by renting out a room on weekends or holidays.
    - Success requires good photos, prompt communication, and a clean space.
    - Airbnb and Vrbo make listing and managing rentals user-friendly.
5. **Wholesaling Real Estate:**
    - Involves finding deeply discounted properties, getting them under contract, and then selling that contract to another investor for a profit.
    - No need to own the property. This is a strategy that requires hustle and a good understanding of your local market.
    - Learning resources include YouTube channels like Max Maxwell or BiggerPockets podcast episodes on wholesaling.

Where to Start:

- **BiggerPockets.com:** The largest online community of real estate investors. Includes forums, calculators, success stories, and a podcast.

- **Local Real Estate Meetups:** Use Meetup.com to find groups in your area. Networking with other investors is a huge advantage.
- **Books to Read:**
    - "Rich Dad Poor Dad" by Robert Kiyosaki
    - "The Book on Rental Property Investing" by Brandon Turner
    - "Set for Life" by Scott Trench

Financing Options:

- **FHA Loan:** 3.5% down payment for owner-occupants.
- **Conventional Loan:** Typically requires 20% down but offers more flexibility.
- **VA Loan:** 0% down payment if you're a veteran.
- **Hard Money Lenders:** Short-term loans based on property value. Useful for flips but come with higher interest rates.

Pros and Cons:

Pros:

- Steady cash flow
- Leverage: control a large asset with little money down

- Tax benefits: depreciation, mortgage interest deductions
- Appreciation over time

Cons:

- Property management headaches – unless you outsource it. Outsourcing comes with greater costs, but worth it if you don't have the skills to do it yourself.
- Tenant turnover and vacancies
- Upfront capital required for down payments and repairs

Investing in Yourself

While stocks, real estate, and retirement accounts build wealth, investing in yourself builds the capacity to earn more, think smarter, and navigate life more effectively. It's the most direct way to upgrade your income potential.

1. Develop New Skills

- Learning skills with high market demand can dramatically increase your earning power.
- **Examples:**
  - Learn Excel or data analysis through free courses on Coursera or Khan Academy.
  - Take copywriting, graphic design, or digital marketing courses on Udemy or Skillshare.

  - For trades, look into certifications in HVAC, electrical, or plumbing at local community colleges.

- **Where to Start:**
  - Coursera.org, edX.org, and YouTube for free education.
  - LinkedIn Learning and Udemy for career-focused courses.
  - Check with local workforce development centers for subsidized classes.

2. Improve Communication Skills

- Being able to express ideas clearly can improve job performance, leadership potential, and networking opportunities.
- **How to Start:**
  - Join a local Toastmasters club.
  - Practice public speaking by volunteering to lead meetings or discussions.
  - Read "Talk Like TED" or "How to Win Friends and Influence People."

3. Build a Personal Brand

- Your online presence can open doors. Whether you're freelancing, job-hunting, or launching a business, people need to find and trust you.

- **Examples:**
    - Start a simple blog or YouTube channel on a topic you're learning.
    - Update your LinkedIn profile to highlight achievements and skills.
    - Share helpful content or case studies related to your profession.

4. Health and Energy Investments

- Your physical health affects your earning power. Poor health reduces productivity and limits options.
- **Practical Steps:**
    - Commit to 30 minutes of walking daily.
    - Cook meals at home instead of relying on fast food.
    - Sleep 7-8 hours per night to maximize mental focus.
- **Why It Matters:**
    - More energy = better performance = more income.

5. Reading and Continuous Learning

- The most successful people are readers. They treat their minds like elite athletes treat their bodies.

- **Books to Start With:**
    - "The Millionaire Fastlane" by MJ DeMarco
    - "Deep Work" by Cal Newport
    - "Atomic Habits" by James Clear
    - "So Good They Can't Ignore You" by Cal Newport

6. Get a Mentor or Join a Mastermind Group

- Learning from others' experience shortens your learning curve and prevents expensive mistakes.
- **How to Start:**
    - Reach out to someone in your field and ask for a short Zoom chat.
    - Join Facebook groups or LinkedIn communities for your interest area.
    - Attend conferences or webinars—even virtual ones—to connect with like-minded people.

7. Side Hustle Practice

- Starting a small business or side hustle—even if it doesn't earn much at first—can teach skills that last a lifetime.

- **Ideas:**
    - Sell homemade items on Etsy.
    - Start a small blog that recommends products (affiliate marketing).
    - Offer tutoring or resume review services online.

Why This Matters

Investing in yourself builds confidence, competence, and career capital. These are the assets that allow you to pivot, seize opportunities, and bounce back from setbacks. Unlike the stock market, these investments never lose value—they appreciate as you do.

Avoiding Common Investment Mistakes

Most people lose money in the market not because the investments are bad, but because they make poor decisions at the wrong times. Understanding these mistakes and learning how to avoid them can save you years of frustration.

1. Trying to Time the Market

- Many investors try to guess when the market will rise or fall. Even professionals rarely succeed at this.
- **Example:** Someone pulls their money out during a dip and misses the rebound. They sell low and buy back high.

- **Better Approach:** Stick to a consistent investment schedule and focus on long-term performance. Use dollar-cost averaging to reduce timing risk.

2. Chasing Hot Stocks or Trends

- It's tempting to buy into the latest hype—whether it's tech stocks, meme stocks, or cryptocurrency.
- **Example:** Buying into a trending stock after it has already surged in price, only to watch it crash.
- **How to Avoid:** Research before you invest. Ask: "What is this company's long-term value?" Avoid decisions based on social media or fear of missing out (FOMO).

3. Failing to Diversify

- Putting all your money into one stock or one asset class increases your risk significantly.
- **Example:** Someone invests only in tech stocks. When tech crashes, they lose half their portfolio.
- **Smart Strategy:** Spread your investments across industries, asset classes (stocks, bonds, real estate), and even international markets using index funds or ETF.

4. Not Understanding What You're Investing In

- If you can't explain what a company or investment does, you shouldn't put money into it.
- **Example:** Many people invested in Enron or Theranos without understanding the business. Both collapsed due to fraud.
- **Tip:** Stick to businesses or industries you can understand. Read the basics—start with a company's website, recent news articles, and earnings summaries.

5. Letting Emotions Drive Decisions

- Fear and greed are the two biggest enemies of long-term investing.
- **Common Scenario:** When the market drops, panic leads people to sell. When the market soars, greed leads them to buy overpriced stocks.
- **What to Do:** Create a plan and stick to it. Automate your investments and check your portfolio no more than once a quarter unless needed.

6. Ignoring Fees

- Fees eat into your returns over time. Even a 1% difference in fees can cost you tens of thousands of dollars over decades.
- **Example:** Paying 1.5% to a mutual fund manager versus 0.04% for a low-cost index fund like those from Vanguard or Fidelity.

- **How to Reduce Fees:** Choose low-cost ETFs or index funds. Avoid unnecessary trading. Use fee-free brokers like Fidelity, Schwab, or Vanguard.

7. Not Reinvesting Dividends

- Dividends are a significant part of long-term returns, especially with dividend-paying stocks.
- **Mistake:** Taking dividends as cash instead of reinvesting.
- **Better Strategy:** Choose "dividend reinvestment" in your brokerage account. It boosts your compounding power.

8. Lack of a Written Plan

- Many people invest without a clear goal or strategy.
- **Problem:** Without a plan, you're more likely to react emotionally.
- **Solution:** Write out a simple plan: What are you investing for? What is your time horizon? What risk level are you comfortable with?

9. Starting Too Late

- The longer you wait, the harder it is to catch up.
- **Example:** Someone who waits until 40 to start investing will have to contribute nearly three times more per month than someone who starts at 25 to reach the same goal.

- **Action Step:** Start with what you can. Even $25 a month matters. Use apps like Acorns or Fidelity's no-minimum investment funds.

A Simple Starter Portfolio

You don't need a finance degree or a Wall Street advisor to start investing. Many successful investors begin with a basic portfolio built on proven, low-cost strategies. The key is to keep it simple and consistent.

Start With the S&P 500

The following strategy worked for me, but it may not work for you! I am in no way giving you investment advice - only telling you what worked for me! **You must invest at your own risk and you may lose money with any investment you make. I am not responsible for any losses or gains you make in the market!**

With that disclaimer out of the way, a great place to begin is by investing in a fund that tracks the S&P 500. This index includes 500 of the largest and most stable companies in the U.S., such as Apple, Microsoft, Amazon, and Johnson & Johnson. Over the past century, the S&P 500 has delivered an average annual return of about 10% before inflation.

Why the S&P 500?

- It's diversified across industries.
- It's low-cost and accessible.
- It's proven to outperform most actively managed funds over time.

How to Invest in the S&P 500

You can start investing in an S&P 500 index fund or ETF (Exchange Traded Fund) through any major brokerage firm.

Top Choices:

- **Vanguard S&P 500 ETF (VOO)** – Known for its extremely low expense ratio (~0.03%).
- **Fidelity 500 Index Fund (FXAIX)** – No minimum investment and also low cost.
- **Schwab S&P 500 Index Fund (SWPPX)** – Great for beginners with no fees to start.

How to Get Started:

1. **Open a Brokerage Account:**
    - Use platforms like Fidelity, Vanguard, Schwab, or even apps like M1 Finance or SoFi.
    - Choose one with no fees and user-friendly navigation.
2. **Link Your Bank Account:**
    - Set up automatic transfers each month. Start small if needed—$25, $50, or $100 a month.
3. **Buy the Fund:**
    - Search for the ticker symbol (like VOO, FXAIX, or SWPPX) and purchase shares.

- ○ Choose to reinvest dividends to maximize compounding.

4. **Stay Consistent:**

- ○ Don't try to time the market. Keep contributing monthly. Let time do the heavy lifting.

Conclusion: It's Not About Timing, It's About Time

Smart investing doesn't require a perfect strategy or timing the market. It requires a commitment to consistency, a willingness to learn, and patience to let time and compound growth do their work. Anyone—even someone starting with modest means—can build real wealth by focusing on the fundamentals covered in this chapter.

By now, you've seen that it's entirely possible to begin investing with limited income and still make progress toward long-term financial goals. You've learned the importance of retirement accounts, the accessibility of index funds like those tracking the S&P 500, and the need to avoid common mistakes that can derail your momentum.

In the next chapter, we'll explore how to protect what you've built. Wealth isn't just about growing your money—it's also about shielding it from unnecessary risk, unexpected emergencies, and poor decision-making. Chapter 5 will cover emergency funds, insurance, estate planning, and more. These are critical components of financial security that too often get overlooked, but they're just as important as investing wisely. Let's move from offense to defense and build a financial plan that can weather whatever life throws at you.

Chapter 5: Protecting Your Wealth

Building wealth is just one part of the equation. The other part is safeguarding it. Wealth creation is a long-term journey that requires not just smart investments but also a solid plan for managing risks, protecting against unforeseen events, and ensuring your assets are secure. Whether you're just starting or you've accumulated some savings, it's important to address these protective measures to avoid unnecessary losses.

In this chapter, we'll explore how to protect your financial future with emergency funds, insurance, estate planning, and the steps you can take to ensure your wealth is shielded from potential threats.

Emergency Funds: The Foundation of Financial Security

An emergency fund is the first and most important layer of protection. It's your financial safety net for unforeseen situations, such as medical emergencies, job loss, or urgent home repairs. Without an emergency fund, even small unexpected costs can derail your financial progress.

Why an Emergency Fund Matters:

- It keeps you from going into debt when life throws a curveball.
- It provides peace of mind, knowing you have resources available when needed.

- It allows you to make thoughtful decisions in tough situations rather than acting out of financial desperation.

How Much Should You Save? Financial experts typically recommend setting aside three to six months' worth of living expenses in an emergency fund. If you have a steady income and limited expenses, three months may be sufficient. However, if you are self-employed or work in a job with inconsistent income, aim for six months or more.

Where to Keep Your Emergency Fund: Your emergency fund should be easily accessible, but it shouldn't be so accessible that you're tempted to dip into it for non-emergencies. A high-yield savings account or a money market account is ideal. These accounts allow you to earn some interest while keeping your funds safe and accessible.

Steps to Build Your Emergency Fund:

1. **Set a Goal:** Calculate how much you need to cover your essential expenses (housing, food, utilities, transportation, insurance, etc.).

2. **Start Small:** If you're just getting started, begin with a smaller goal—$500 or $1,000—and build from there.

3. **Automate Contributions:** Set up automatic transfers from your checking account into your emergency savings to ensure consistency.

4. **Prioritize Savings:** Consider your emergency fund a priority. Before making additional investments, ensure your fund is fully established.

Insurance: Protecting Your Wealth from the Unexpected

Insurance is a form of risk management that provides financial protection in case something goes wrong. It's the safety net that helps you recover when things fall apart, whether it's your health, car, home, or life.

Types of Insurance to Consider:

1. **Health Insurance:**
   - Health insurance is essential to protect yourself from the high costs of medical treatment. Without it, you could face crushing medical bills in case of an accident, illness, or long-term health condition.
   - Even with health insurance, make sure to understand your deductible, co-pays, and out-of-pocket limits.
2. **Life Insurance:**
   - If you have dependents or family members who rely on your income, life insurance is crucial. It ensures that your family is financially protected if something were to happen to you.
   - There are two main types of life insurance: term life (coverage for a set period) and whole life (permanent coverage with an investment component).

- Term life insurance is often sufficient for those just starting out and can be obtained at a reasonable rate.

3. **Auto Insurance:**

   - Auto insurance is a legal requirement in most states, but it also protects you financially if you're in an accident or your car is damaged.
   - Review your coverage to ensure you have enough protection. Consider both liability and comprehensive coverage for full protection.

4. **Homeowners or Renters Insurance:**

   - Homeowners insurance is vital for protecting your home and belongings against damage from events such as fire, theft, or natural disasters.
   - Renters insurance, while often overlooked, can protect your personal property and cover liability in case of accidents or damage within your rental.

5. **Disability Insurance:**

   - Disability insurance replaces a portion of your income if you become unable to work due to illness or injury. This coverage is especially important for individuals who rely solely on their paycheck.

  - Consider short-term and long-term disability insurance to cover different scenarios.

How to Choose the Right Insurance:

- **Assess Your Needs:** Look at your financial situation, dependents, and lifestyle. The more at-risk your financial situation is, the more insurance you need.

- **Get Multiple Quotes:** Insurance prices can vary widely, so shop around for the best rates while ensuring you have enough coverage.

- **Review Regularly:** As your circumstances change—such as getting married, having children, or buying a home—make sure your insurance coverage is adjusted accordingly.

Estate Planning: Protecting Your Wealth for Future Generations

Estate planning is not just for the wealthy; it's for anyone who wants to ensure their assets are distributed according to their wishes after they're gone. Without a plan, your assets could be tied up in court, and your loved ones may face a lengthy, stressful process.

Key Components of Estate Planning:

1. **Will:** A will outlines how your property and assets will be distributed after your death. It can also name guardians for your children, should the worst happen.

- Without a will, your assets could be distributed by the state, potentially against your wishes.
- Consider working with an estate attorney to ensure your will is legally valid and covers all necessary elements.

2. **Trusts:** A trust allows you to place assets into a legal entity that can be managed on behalf of beneficiaries. A trust can avoid the probate process, providing quicker access to your assets and reducing tax burdens.
    - Trusts are especially useful for people with significant assets or those who want to leave money to minors or family members with special needs.
3. **Durable Power of Attorney:** This document gives someone you trust the authority to make financial decisions on your behalf if you become incapacitated.
4. **Healthcare Power of Attorney:** This is similar to a durable power of attorney, but it allows someone to make medical decisions for you if you are unable to do so yourself.
5. **Beneficiary Designations:** Many assets—such as life insurance policies, retirement accounts, and bank accounts—allow you to designate a beneficiary. These designations take precedence over your will, so it's important to keep them up-to-date.

Steps to Get Started with Estate Planning:

1. **Start with a Will:** Make sure your will is clear, legal, and up to date.

2. **Consider a Trust:** If you have assets you want to manage or transfer in a specific way, a trust may be right for you.

3. **Review Beneficiary Designations:** Double-check your life insurance and retirement accounts to ensure your beneficiaries are current.

4. **Consult an Attorney:** An estate planning lawyer can help you navigate complex issues, especially if you have a substantial estate.

Keeping Your Wealth Safe from Scams and Frauds

Financial scams and frauds are becoming more prevalent, and the consequences of falling victim to one can be devastating. Protecting yourself involves vigilance and understanding how scams typically work. **IF ANYONE EVER ASKS YOU TO PAY WITH GIFT CARDS, IT IS A SCAM!**

Common Scams to Avoid:

- **Investment Scams:** Be wary of "too good to be true" investment opportunities, especially those that promise high returns with little risk. Always research the company and speak with a financial advisor before making decisions.

- **Phishing Scams:** These involve fraudulent emails or phone calls from people posing as legitimate organizations asking for personal information. Always double-check the source of communication and never give out sensitive information over the phone.

- **Ponzi Schemes:** These scams promise high returns, but they pay earlier investors with the money from newer investors. They eventually collapse when new investors stop joining.

How to Protect Yourself:

The landscape of personal finance is riddled with risks, and scams are one of the most significant threats to your wealth. Whether it's a fraudulent investment scheme, identity theft, or phishing attempts, scammers prey on individuals who aren't informed about how to identify and protect themselves from these tactics.

Understanding Common Scams

1. **Investment Scams: How to Protect Yourself:** Always do your due diligence before committing money to an investment. Be wary of unsolicited offers, and research the company or opportunity thoroughly. Check the background of the individuals offering the investment by using resources like the SEC's EDGAR database and state securities regulators.

    - Investment scams promise high returns with little or no risk, a combination that rarely exists. Common scams include Ponzi schemes, where the returns to earlier investors are paid with the money of new investors rather than through legitimate profits, and high-risk investments that are disguised as low-risk opportunities.

- Example: A person promises you a 20% return on a "guaranteed" investment in a short period of time. If it sounds too good to be true, it usually is.

2. **Phishing Scams: How to Protect Yourself:** Be cautious of emails or messages asking for personal information. Do not click on links in unsolicited emails. Instead, go directly to the website by typing the address into your browser. Enable two-factor authentication (2FA) on all accounts to add an extra layer of security.

    - Phishing involves fraudulent communications (usually via email) designed to trick you into providing sensitive personal information, such as login credentials, Social Security numbers, or credit card details. Scammers may pose as legitimate companies, banks, or government agencies.

    - Example: You receive an email claiming to be from your bank, asking you to click a link to verify your account or "update" your details. The link redirects you to a fake website where you enter your login information, which the scammer can then steal.

3. **Ponzi Schemes and High-Yield Investment Programs (HYIPs): How to Protect Yourself:** Recognize red flags like promises of high returns with little to no risk. Research the investment thoroughly and be skeptical of any investment opportunities that pressure you into making decisions quickly or without time for due diligence.

   - A Ponzi scheme is a type of investment scam where the returns to early investors are paid using the contributions of new investors rather than from profits earned. Eventually, the scheme collapses when new investors stop joining, leaving latecomers with significant losses.

   - Example: A so-called "high-yield investment program" promises returns that far exceed typical market returns, often 10%-20% per month. These schemes typically operate without any legal registration and offer no real underlying assets.

4. **Lottery or Prize Scams: How to Protect Yourself:** Never pay money upfront to claim a prize. If you didn't enter a contest, it's likely a scam. Be cautious of unsolicited offers, especially those that ask for money or personal details in exchange for a reward.

   - These scams inform you that you've won a lottery or prize that you never entered. They often require an upfront fee for taxes, delivery charges, or handling before you can claim your "winnings."

- Example: You receive an email or text stating you've won a foreign lottery and need to pay a fee to collect your prize.

5. **Romance Scams: How to Protect Yourself:** Avoid sending money to someone you haven't met in person, even if you've been communicating online for a long time. Be especially cautious of anyone asking for money for emergency reasons, as this is a common tactic used by scammers.

    - Romance scams occur when a fraudster builds an online relationship with someone and eventually asks for money, often under the pretense of a personal emergency, travel expenses, or other fabricated scenarios.

    - Example: After exchanging messages online, someone you've never met may start asking for money to cover an "emergency" while pretending to have feelings for you.

Scammer Payback: A Real-World Example of Fighting Back

One effective resource for exposing and educating the public about scams is the YouTube channel **Scammer Payback**. Hosted by a security researcher and ethical hacker, the channel has garnered attention for its entertaining and educational approach to tackling scammers head-on. The host uses a combination of technical know-how, investigative work, and social engineering to expose scammers and waste their time—often with humor and wit.

How Scammer Payback Works: The host engages with scammers, often posing as a victim or someone with potential access to funds, to gather information and waste their time. Through this process, he not only disrupts the scammer's operations but also educates his audience about the tactics used in these schemes. The channel showcases real-life examples of how scammers work and provides viewers with actionable tips on how to protect themselves from these types of fraud.

Key Lessons from Scammer Payback:

1. **Stay Calm:** If you receive a scam phone call or email, the best response is to remain calm and don't panic. Scammers often use high-pressure tactics to rush you into making decisions.

2. **Know the Red Flags:** Scammer Payback regularly points out red flags, such as unsolicited contact, promises of large sums of money, or threats of dire consequences if you don't act immediately.

3. **Take Your Time:** Scammers often try to rush you into making quick decisions. Never feel pressured to act quickly—take your time to research, verify, and think things through.

4. **Use Technology to Your Advantage:** Scammer Payback demonstrates how tech tools like reverse number lookups, virtual machines, and caller ID apps can help protect against scams and identify fraudulent activity.

While the primary goal of Scammer Payback is to entertain, the channel also serves as a vital public service. Watching the host interact with scammers can help viewers recognize the common techniques used to manipulate and defraud people. The channel is a great resource for those who want to learn more about how scammers operate and how to avoid falling victim to their schemes.

Actionable Steps to Protect Yourself:

1. **Watch Videos:** Scammer Payback and other similar YouTube channels can give you real-time examples of how scammers operate. Pay close attention to the signs they highlight and familiarize yourself with the common tricks.

2. **Use Technology:** Install anti-virus software, use secure browsing habits, and enable two-factor authentication on your accounts to add extra layers of protection.

3. **Report Suspicious Activity:** If you come across a scam, report it to the authorities. For example, the Federal Trade Commission (FTC) in the U.S. has an easy-to-use website to report fraud and scams.

General Tips for Protecting Your Wealth from Scams:

- **Verify the Source:** Always check the legitimacy of any offers, especially when they come from unknown or unverified sources. Look up company names, contact details, and reviews from trusted sites.

- **Educate Yourself and Others:** Stay up-to-date on the latest scams and fraud tactics. Share this knowledge with your friends and family to prevent them from falling victim.

- **Use Strong, Unique Passwords:** Make sure your passwords are not easy to guess and use different passwords for each of your accounts.

- **Be Wary of Unsolicited Calls and Emails:** Never share personal information with anyone who contacts you out of the blue. If the person is truly legitimate, they will not ask for sensitive information over unsecured channels.

Conclusion

Protecting your wealth from scams requires constant vigilance. Understanding the tactics used by fraudsters, securing your personal information, and learning how to respond to suspicious activity can go a long way in preserving your financial security. By following the advice in this chapter, and taking the time to educate yourself through resources like **Scammer Payback**, you'll be better prepared to spot fraud before it affects you.

Now that you've laid the groundwork—cutting costs with intention, growing your income through strategy, and making smart investments—it's time to zoom out and look at the big picture. In this next chapter, we'll revisit key concepts like the importance of long-term planning, how the 50/30/20 rule can guide your everyday financial decisions, and why protecting what you've built matters just as much as building it. We'll take a practical look at insurance, estate planning, and other tools that help safeguard your future. This chapter is about pulling everything together into a cohesive plan—one that helps you not just grow wealth, but protect it for the long haul. Be sure to review the material, even though we've covered it in previous chapters!

Chapter 6: Reviewing What We Have Learned So Far

A long-term financial plan is the cornerstone of building and preserving wealth. While short-term goals are important for immediate financial needs, long-term planning ensures that you have the resources to achieve your bigger dreams. It serves as a roadmap, helping you stay focused on your goals while navigating the inevitable financial ups and downs that come with life. This chapter will provide you with practical guidance on how to create and maintain a long-term financial plan, and why it is crucial for building wealth on a modest income.

Why Long-Term Planning Matters

Many people focus on short-term financial goals: paying off credit card debt, building an emergency fund, or saving for a vacation. These goals are important, but they don't provide a solid foundation for long-term financial stability. Long-term financial planning goes beyond meeting immediate needs and aims to set you up for a secure future. By making long-term decisions now, you can create a path that leads to financial independence and a comfortable retirement.

Long-term planning provides clarity on how to allocate your resources efficiently, invest for the future, and protect your wealth against unforeseen challenges. Whether it's planning for your child's education, saving for retirement, or building a legacy, a long-term financial plan is necessary to achieve these goals.

Key Components of a Long-Term Financial Plan

Creating a comprehensive long-term financial plan involves several key steps. These steps help you establish a clear picture of where you are financially and how to get where you want to go.

1. **Setting Clear Financial Goals**

    - **Define Your Long-Term Objectives:** Begin by identifying what you want to achieve financially over the next 10, 20, or even 30 years. This can include goals like buying a home, starting a business, traveling the world, or retiring early.

    - **Break Down Your Goals:** Once you've set your big-picture goals, break them down into smaller, actionable steps. For example, if your goal is to save for retirement, you can set smaller targets for how much you need to save each month or year to reach your desired retirement fund.

    - **Review and Adjust:** Your goals may change over time as your circumstances evolve. Periodically revisit your financial goals to ensure they still align with your life plans.

2. **Budgeting for the Long-Term: Remember the 50/30/20 rule on expenses**

    - **Track Your Spending:** To make progress toward your long-term goals, you need to understand where your money is going. Create a budget that tracks your income and expenses, and identify areas where you can reduce costs.

    - **Prioritize Savings:** One of the best ways to ensure your financial success is to prioritize savings. Try to automate your savings by setting up automatic transfers to your savings or investment accounts each time you receive a paycheck.

    - **Reduce Debt:** High-interest debt, like credit card debt, can be a major obstacle to achieving your long-term financial goals. Focus on paying off debt as quickly as possible to free up more resources for savings and investment.

3. **Creating a Comprehensive Investment Strategy**

    - **Understand Risk and Return:** Every investment carries a level of risk, and understanding how to balance risk with potential return is crucial to building wealth. Risk tolerance varies from person to person based on factors like age, income, and personal comfort level.

- **Diversification:** A key element of a successful long-term investment strategy is diversification. Spread your investments across different asset classes—stocks, bonds, real estate, and commodities—to minimize risk and maximize returns.

- **Retirement Accounts:** Contribute regularly to retirement accounts such as a 401(k) or Roth IRA. These accounts provide tax advantages and help you build wealth over time. The earlier you start, the more time your investments have to grow.

- **Index Funds and ETFs:** For those who prefer a more hands-off approach, index funds and exchange-traded funds (ETFs) are great options. These funds track the performance of a specific index, like the S&P 500, and provide broad market exposure without the need for individual stock picking.

- **Rebalancing:** Over time, the value of your investments will fluctuate. Rebalancing your portfolio regularly ensures that your asset allocation stays aligned with your risk tolerance and long-term goals.

4. **Building an Emergency Fund**

   - **The Importance of an Emergency Fund:** Life is unpredictable. An emergency fund acts as a financial cushion in case of unexpected events, like a job loss, medical emergency, or major home repair. Aim to save at least three to six months' worth of living expenses in an easily accessible account.

- **How to Build an Emergency Fund:** Start by setting small, manageable savings targets. Even if you can only save $50 per month, the key is consistency. Over time, these small contributions will add up to a substantial emergency fund.

- **Use High-Interest Savings Accounts:** Keep your emergency fund in a high-yield savings account, where it can earn interest while remaining easily accessible.

5. **Protecting Your Wealth with Insurance**

   - **Life Insurance:** If you have dependents or a spouse who relies on your income, life insurance is essential. It provides financial protection to your loved ones in case of your unexpected death. Consider term life insurance, which is typically more affordable and provides coverage for a set period (e.g., 20 years).

   - **Health Insurance:** Medical expenses can be a major financial burden, especially in the case of an unexpected illness or accident. Make sure you have adequate health insurance coverage to protect yourself and your family.

- **Disability Insurance:** Disability insurance provides income replacement if you become unable to work due to illness or injury. It's especially important if you rely on your income to meet your financial obligations.

- **Home and Auto Insurance:** Protect your assets by maintaining appropriate coverage for your home, car, and other valuable property. This type of insurance safeguards you against potential financial losses from accidents or damage.

6. **Tax Planning**

    - **Understand Your Tax Liability:** Taxes can take a significant portion of your income, but with the right planning, you can minimize your tax liability and keep more of what you earn. Consult with a tax professional to explore ways to reduce your taxes, such as through tax-deferred retirement accounts or tax-efficient investment strategies.

    - **Tax-Efficient Investment Strategies:** Certain investment accounts, such as Roth IRAs, allow you to avoid paying taxes on your gains. Be mindful of tax implications when making investment decisions, especially when you're buying or selling assets in taxable accounts.

7. **Estate Planning**

    - **Wills and Trusts:** Estate planning is an often-overlooked aspect of long-term financial planning. Having a will ensures that your assets are distributed according to your wishes when you pass away. Trusts can help manage your estate in a way that reduces estate taxes and provides for your heirs.

    - **Power of Attorney and Health Directives:** These legal documents give someone you trust the authority to make decisions on your behalf if you become incapacitated. They ensure that your financial and healthcare wishes are carried out in your absence.

    - **Review Your Estate Plan Regularly:** As your financial situation changes, so should your estate plan. Review it regularly to ensure that it reflects your current assets, wishes, and the needs of your family.

8. **Regularly Review Your Financial Plan**

    - **Track Your Progress:** Long-term financial planning isn't a set-it-and-forget-it process. Review your plan regularly—at least once a year—to track your progress and make adjustments as needed.

    - **Adapt to Life Changes:** Major life events, such as marriage, having children, or changing jobs, can significantly impact your financial situation. Make sure to update your plan accordingly.

- **Stay Flexible:** Life doesn't always go according to plan. Be prepared to adjust your goals and strategies as needed. Flexibility is key to maintaining a long-term financial plan that works for you.

Conclusion

A long-term financial plan is your blueprint for success. It helps you make informed decisions, stay disciplined in your saving and investing habits, and ultimately reach your financial goals. While the process requires effort and patience, the rewards are well worth it. By following the steps outlined in this chapter, you'll be able to create a comprehensive plan that puts you on the path to financial independence and security.

With the pieces in place—spending smart, earning more, investing wisely, and planning for the future—the next step is learning to stick with it. This chapter is all about financial discipline: the habits, mindset, and daily decisions that keep your financial goals on track. Discipline isn't about saying no to everything fun—it's about staying focused on what you really want and building consistency over time. We'll talk about how to avoid impulse spending, stick to your budget, stay patient during market ups and downs, and develop the kind of long-term thinking that separates wishful saving from real wealth building.

Chapter 7: Mastering Financial Discipline

Now for the hard part... Maintaining discipline with your finances is difficult at best. One of the most important factors in building wealth on a modest income is financial discipline. It's not just about knowing what to do but about consistently doing it. **Building wealth is a long-term process that requires dedication, patience, and a strong commitment to making the right financial decisions every day**. This chapter will dive into the concept of financial discipline—why it's critical for long-term success, how to cultivate it, and practical tips for staying on track.

What is Financial Discipline?

Financial discipline is the ability to stick to a financial plan and make decisions that align with long-term wealth-building goals, even when faced with temptation or short-term gratification. It's the skill of prioritizing your future well-being over immediate desires, which can be difficult in a world full of marketing, credit card offers, and easy access to debt.

Being disciplined in your finances means living within your means, saving and investing consistently, and avoiding impulsive purchases. It involves saying no to things that don't contribute to your long-term financial success while saying yes to practices that will help you get closer to your goals. While financial discipline is often associated with delayed gratification, it's also about knowing when to reward yourself for staying on track and celebrating small victories along the way.

Why Financial Discipline is Crucial for Building Wealth

Building wealth on a modest income is a challenge, but it's not impossible. The key to overcoming that challenge is financial discipline. Without it, the best plans and strategies will fall apart. Here's why financial discipline is so important:

1. **Maximizes the Power of Compound Interest**: By consistently saving and investing, you can take advantage of compound interest, which is the ability of your money to grow exponentially over time. Small amounts invested regularly can accumulate into significant sums over the years, but only if you stay disciplined in your approach.

2. **Keeps You Focused on Long-Term Goals**: Financial discipline helps you resist the temptation to spend on things that are not aligned with your long-term objectives. By sticking to your goals, you keep your eye on the prize, whether that's financial independence, early retirement, or simply living debt-free.

3. **Prevents Financial Setbacks**: Impulse spending, poor investment choices, and taking on excessive debt can derail your financial journey. Financial discipline allows you to avoid these common pitfalls and keep your wealth-building efforts on course.

4. **Increases Financial Confidence**: When you practice financial discipline, you gain control over your money. This leads to greater confidence in your financial decision-making and a deeper understanding of how to manage and grow your wealth.

How to Cultivate Financial Discipline

Financial discipline is a habit, and like any habit, it takes time and effort to develop. The good news is that once you develop these habits, they will start working for you, leading to positive financial results over time. Here are some strategies to help you cultivate financial discipline:

1. **Set Clear, Achievable Goals**

    - **Long-Term Goals**: Start with clear long-term goals—saving for retirement, buying a home, or creating an emergency fund. These goals should align with your values and be something that excites you.

    - **Short-Term Milestones**: Break your long-term goals into smaller, manageable milestones. This makes your goals less overwhelming and provides more frequent opportunities to celebrate progress.

    - **Track Your Progress**: Use financial tools or apps to track your spending and savings progress. Seeing your achievements helps keep you motivated and reinforces your commitment to your goals.

2. **Create a Detailed Budget**

   - **Live Below Your Means**: One of the most effective ways to build wealth on a modest income is to live below your means. Create a budget that reflects your current income and expenses, and prioritize savings.

   - **Automate Savings**: Set up automatic transfers to savings and investment accounts so that you don't have to think about it. This ensures that you are saving first, before spending on discretionary items.

   - **Budget for Fun**: Financial discipline doesn't mean complete deprivation. It's about balance. Set aside money for entertainment and leisure activities, but be mindful of how much you spend.

3. **Practice Delayed Gratification**

   - **Focus on Long-Term Rewards**: Building wealth takes time, and you won't see immediate results. It's important to stay focused on the long-term rewards of your financial discipline—whether it's the peace of mind that comes with being debt-free or the ability to retire comfortably.

   - **Evaluate Your Spending**: Before making purchases, ask yourself whether the item or experience is aligned with your financial goals. Can you delay the purchase, or is it something you really need right now? This simple practice helps curb impulse spending.

4. **Track Your Spending and Cut Unnecessary Costs**

   - **Audit Your Expenses**: Regularly track your spending to identify areas where you can cut back. Do you really need that subscription service? Are there cheaper alternatives for some of your regular expenses? Every dollar saved is one more dollar that can go toward your financial goals.

   - **Avoid Lifestyle Inflation**: As your income increases, it's tempting to increase your spending as well. However, the key to building wealth is to maintain your lifestyle while increasing your savings rate. Instead of upgrading your lifestyle with every pay raise, consider saving or investing the extra income.

5. **Stay Accountable**

   - **Find an Accountability Partner**: Share your financial goals with a trusted friend or family member who can help hold you accountable. Regular check-ins can provide motivation and prevent you from straying off track.

   - **Use Technology**: Financial apps can help you monitor your progress and stay on top of your goals. Apps like Mint or YNAB (You Need a Budget) provide insight into your spending habits, helping you stay disciplined.

- **Celebrate Small Wins**: Financial discipline doesn't have to be all about sacrifice. Take time to celebrate small milestones along the way, whether that's paying off a credit card or hitting a savings target. Positive reinforcement helps maintain motivation.

6. **Commit to Lifelong Learning**

   - **Educate Yourself**: Continually learning about personal finance, investing, and money management can help strengthen your discipline. There's always more to learn, and staying informed ensures that you're making the best possible financial decisions.

   - **Read Books and Watch Videos**: Seek out resources like books, and YouTube channels that focus on personal finance and investing. Surrounding yourself with financial education will make it easier to stay disciplined.

Practical Tips for Maintaining Financial Discipline

1. **Use the 24-Hour Rule**: Before making any large purchase, wait 24 hours to evaluate whether it's something you really need. This simple rule helps prevent impulse buying.

2. **Cut Back on Credit Card Use**: Credit cards are a major temptation for overspending. Try to limit your credit card use to only essential purchases, and always pay your balance in full each month.

3. **Set Financial Boundaries**: Set limits on how much you'll spend each month (e.g., dining out, entertainment, shopping). If you reach the limit, resist the temptation to spend more.

4. **Avoid "Keeping Up with the Joneses"**: Social pressure can be strong, but it's important to remember that everyone's financial journey is different. Avoid comparing your financial situation to others, and instead focus on your own progress and goals.

Overcoming Challenges to Financial Discipline

Financial discipline is not easy. Life can throw unexpected challenges your way—job loss, medical emergencies, or unforeseen expenses can make it harder to stick to your plan. However, it's during these times that your discipline is most important. Here are some strategies for overcoming obstacles:

1. **Build a Safety Net**: An emergency fund can provide a buffer in times of crisis, giving you the breathing room to continue making progress toward your goals, even during difficult times.

2. **Be Flexible, Not Complacent**: If you experience a financial setback, don't abandon your long-term goals. Instead, reassess your situation and adjust your budget or savings plan to keep moving forward.

3. **Seek Support**: If you're struggling to stay disciplined, don't be afraid to seek professional help. A financial advisor or coach can provide guidance and accountability, helping you get back on track.

Conclusion

Financial discipline is the foundation of wealth-building. It allows you to make the right choices day after day, despite the temptations and distractions that come your way. While it may not always be easy, staying disciplined in your financial practices will pay off in the long run.

The key to mastering financial discipline is consistency. By setting clear goals, tracking your spending, and making intentional financial decisions, you'll be able to build a strong financial foundation, regardless of your income. Remember, financial discipline is a marathon, not a sprint. Stick with it, and you'll find that your wealth will steadily grow over time.

In the next chapter, we'll take a closer look at the psychology of money and explore how your mindset can impact your ability to build wealth. By understanding the mental and emotional aspects of money, you'll gain a better understanding of how to overcome limiting beliefs and cultivate a wealth-building mindset.

Chapter 8: The Psychology of Money: Mastering Your Mindset for Wealth

Money isn't just about numbers—it's also about mindset. Our beliefs, emotions, and habits shape the way we think about and interact with money. If you want to build wealth, it's essential to address the mental and emotional aspects of financial decision-making. In this chapter, we'll dive into the psychology of money, how your mindset affects your ability to create and maintain wealth, and how to develop the right mental habits to achieve financial success.

Understanding the Role of Mindset in Building Wealth

At its core, the psychology of money is about understanding the way our thoughts and beliefs about money impact our financial decisions. Your mindset can either help you achieve financial success or hold you back. People who have a positive relationship with money—those who view it as a tool to achieve their goals—are generally more successful in managing their finances. On the other hand, those with a negative mindset toward money—seeing it as a source of stress or conflict—often struggle to manage their finances and build wealth.

There are several key mental attitudes that can make a difference when it comes to money:

1. **Scarcity vs. Abundance Mindset**: People with a scarcity mindset believe that money is limited and that there's never enough to go around. They may feel anxious about money, constantly worrying about losing what they have or not having enough. In contrast, those with an abundance mindset see opportunities everywhere and believe that there is plenty of money to be made. They view money as a tool to create positive change in their lives and the lives of others.

2. **Short-Term vs. Long-Term Thinking**: Those who think in the short term may focus on immediate gratification—spending money on things that give instant pleasure but offer no long-term value. Long-term thinkers, however, are willing to delay gratification in order to achieve greater rewards down the road. This kind of thinking is essential for building wealth over time, as it allows you to prioritize saving, investing, and making strategic decisions that benefit your financial future.

3. **Beliefs about Self-Worth and Money**: How you feel about yourself often influences how you handle money. If you believe that you deserve success and wealth, you'll be more likely to take the necessary steps to achieve it. However, if you feel unworthy of wealth or believe that money is inherently bad or unattainable, you may subconsciously sabotage your efforts to build it.

4. **Money as a Source of Stress**: For many, money is a major source of stress and anxiety. Fear of not having enough money, fear of losing what you have, and fear of making the wrong financial deci-

sions can lead to poor choices, procrastination, or even avoidance of financial matters altogether. Learning to manage this stress and shift your mindset is a critical step toward financial freedom.

How to Develop a Wealth-Building Mindset

Your mindset is not fixed—it can be changed and cultivated over time. Here are several strategies for developing a wealth-building mindset that will set you on the path to financial success:

1. **Shift to an Abundance Mindset**

    - **Focus on Opportunities, Not Limitations**: An abundance mindset encourages you to seek out opportunities for growth rather than focusing on the things you lack. Instead of thinking about how hard it is to make money, focus on all the ways you can generate income or create value for others.

    - **Recognize the Power of Choice**: An abundance mindset helps you see that you have choices in your financial life. You can choose to learn, to take action, and to change your financial situation. The more you empower yourself, the more confident you'll feel in your financial decisions.

2. **Embrace Long-Term Thinking**

    - **Set Clear Long-Term Goals**: Building wealth is a long-term endeavor, and it's crucial to develop a clear vision of where you want to be in the future. Whether it's achieving financial independence, retiring early, or simply being debt-free, a long-term goal provides the focus and motivation you need to stay disciplined in your efforts.

  - **Practice Patience**: Wealth doesn't accumulate overnight. In fact, the wealthiest individuals are often those who have been patient and disciplined with their finances over many years or even decades. By committing to your long-term goals, you can avoid the temptation to seek quick, short-term gains that can derail your progress.

3. **Develop a Positive Relationship with Money**

  - **View Money as a Tool**: Instead of seeing money as something to be feared or obsessed over, view it as a tool that can help you achieve your goals. Money allows you to create the life you want, whether that's through investments, business ventures, or philanthropy.

  - **Change Your Money Beliefs**: If you have limiting beliefs about money—such as the idea that "money is the root of all evil" or "rich people are greedy"—you need to reframe those beliefs. Money in itself is neither good nor bad; it's simply a tool. By changing your beliefs about money, you can open up new opportunities for financial growth.

4. **Overcome Money Anxiety**

    - **Track Your Finances**: A major source of financial anxiety is uncertainty. When you don't know where your money is going or how much you have, it's easy to feel overwhelmed. Tracking your spending, savings, and investments helps you feel more in control of your financial situation.

    - **Create an Emergency Fund**: Having an emergency fund provides a financial cushion for unexpected expenses and can reduce anxiety. Knowing that you have a safety net in place allows you to approach your finances with more confidence and less fear.

    - **Seek Support**: If money anxiety is overwhelming you, consider seeking guidance from a financial advisor, counselor, or therapist. Talking about your financial fears can help reduce stress and provide a clearer perspective on your financial situation.

The Impact of Your Financial Beliefs

Your beliefs about money directly influence your financial behavior. If you believe that you will never be able to save enough, that investing is too risky, or that wealthy people are inherently lucky or unethical, you may unconsciously make decisions that keep you from achieving financial success. Conversely, if you believe that you can build wealth and that financial success is within your reach, you are more likely to take action toward your goals.

Here are some common money beliefs that can limit your financial progress—and how to counter them:

1. **"Money is Hard to Make"**: This belief can lead to feelings of frustration. To counter this belief, start by learning about ways to increase your income—whether through side hustles, entrepreneurship, or advancing your career. Realizing that there are many opportunities to make money will shift your perspective and open up possibilities.

2. **"I'm Not Good with Money"**: Many people believe that financial success is only for people with special skills or knowledge. This belief can prevent you from taking the necessary steps to learn about personal finance. To combat this, educate yourself through books, courses, podcasts, or by consulting a financial advisor. Anyone can learn to manage money with the right resources.

3. **"I Don't Deserve Wealth"**: This belief can come from past experiences, cultural messages, or feelings of inadequacy. Overcoming this mindset requires developing a sense of self-worth and recognizing that you are deserving of financial success. Start by focusing on the positive things you've done in your life and how you can use wealth to make a positive impact on others.

4. **"Money Will Solve All My Problems"**: While money can alleviate certain stresses, it isn't a cure-all. Money can provide comfort and security, but it won't solve deeper emotional or personal issues. It's important to balance financial goals with emotional well-being and relationships.

How to Make Better Financial Decisions

A positive mindset doesn't just help you build wealth—it also helps you make better financial decisions. Here's how to ensure that your mental outlook is leading you to sound financial choices:

1. **Avoid Emotional Decision-Making**: Making financial decisions based on emotions—such as fear, greed, or guilt—can lead to poor choices. Practice mindfulness when making financial decisions. Take time to think through your options, do research, and consider the long-term effects of your decisions.

2. **Commit to Continuous Improvement**: Wealth-building is a journey, not a destination. As you grow and learn, you'll encounter new challenges and opportunities. Stay flexible and open to adjusting your plans as necessary. Always look for ways to improve your knowledge and skills, and be willing to learn from mistakes.

3. **Embrace the Power of Consistency**: Building wealth is all about consistency. Whether you're saving for retirement, investing in the stock market, or growing your side hustle, small, consistent actions will compound over time. Trust in the process and continue making progress, even when it feels slow.

Conclusion

Your mindset is the foundation upon which your financial success is built. By developing a wealth-building mindset, you can overcome limiting beliefs, eliminate financial anxiety, and make better decisions that support your goals. Remember, the road to financial success is a marathon, not a sprint. Cultivate patience, embrace long-term thinking, and stay disciplined in your actions.

In the next chapter, we'll explore how cutting costs doesn't have to mean sacrificing the things that bring you joy. It's not about constantly feeling deprived or pinching pennies—it's about making mindful choices and finding creative ways to enjoy life without overspending. We'll dive into strategies for finding low-cost fun, whether it's enjoying nature, exploring free activities in your community, or embracing simple pleasures that don't come with a hefty price tag. By shifting your mindset and being intentional with your purchases, you can enjoy a rich, fulfilling life while still building the financial future you want.

Chapter 9: Cutting Costs Without Sacrificing Happiness

When it comes to building wealth on a modest income, one of the most effective strategies is cutting costs. However, cost-cutting doesn't mean you have to deprive yourself of the things that bring you joy. In fact, with the right mindset, you can achieve financial success without sacrificing your happiness or lifestyle. The key lies in smart spending—finding ways to reduce expenses without feeling like you're missing out on the experiences or pleasures that make life enjoyable.

In this chapter, we'll dive into how to cut costs effectively while maintaining happiness, exploring sustainable frugality, and discovering free or low-cost joys that can enrich your life. We'll also discuss how you can make long-term changes in your spending habits that will not only help you save money but also set you up for financial independence in the future.

Smart Spending vs. Deprivation

When it comes to cutting costs, many people worry that it means living a life of deprivation—cutting out everything that makes life enjoyable or fun. The truth is, cutting costs doesn't have to mean giving up your favorite things. It's about being smarter with how you spend money. Rather than simply slashing expenses in every area, smart spending allows you to keep the things you enjoy while focusing on what's truly important. It's about finding balance and ensuring that you're getting the most out of your spending.

Prioritizing Your Expenses

The first step in smart spending is understanding where your money goes. Breaking down your expenses into categories will help you determine what is truly essential and what can be reduced or eliminated.

Essential Expenses

Your essential expenses are the basics that you can't live without. These are things like:

- **Rent/Mortgage**: This is typically the largest expense for most people. If you're looking to reduce housing costs, consider moving to a less expensive area, downsizing, or looking into rental options that offer better value. If you own a home, refinancing to a lower interest rate might reduce your monthly payment.

- **Utilities**: These include things like electricity, water, internet, and heating. While these are necessary for daily life, they don't have to break the bank. Switching to energy-efficient appliances, using smart thermostats, and being mindful of your usage can help reduce your bills.

- **Transportation**: Whether you own a car or use public transportation, commuting costs can add up quickly. Consider whether public transportation or carpooling can help save you money. If you drive, a more fuel-efficient vehicle might help lower gas costs over time.

- **Food**: Groceries are essential, but they don't have to be expensive. Buying in bulk, choosing generic brands, cooking at home, and meal planning are all strategies that can help you save on food. Additionally, cutting back on eating out can free up more money for savings or investments.

Non-Essential Expenses

These are the things you enjoy but can live without if necessary. Common examples include:

- **Entertainment**: Cable subscriptions, streaming services, and frequent trips to the movies are non-essential but often eat up a large chunk of your budget. Instead of paying for multiple streaming services, consider one or two that offer the content you enjoy. Or, try free options like YouTube or local libraries for movies and shows.

- **Dining Out**: Going to restaurants or ordering takeout adds up fast. It's possible to eat out less often while still enjoying delicious meals. Meal prep and cooking at home is much cheaper, and you can recreate your favorite restaurant meals for a fraction of the price.

- **Shopping**: Clothes, gadgets, and other impulse purchases are often driven by trends and the desire for instant gratification. While it's fun to buy new things, these types of purchases don't add long-term value to your life. Instead, focus on quality over quantity, and be selective with your purchases.

Value Over Quantity

One of the most powerful aspects of smart spending is focusing on value rather than quantity. This doesn't mean avoiding fun or rewarding yourself—it means spending your money in ways that bring you the most satisfaction and fulfillment.

Invest in Durability

Buying quality items that last longer will save you money in the long run. For example, instead of buying cheap clothes that wear out after a few months, invest in well-made garments that will last for years. This applies to everything from shoes to kitchen appliances. Higher-quality items may cost more upfront, but their longevity means you won't have to replace them as often.

- **Example**: If you need a new pair of boots, instead of buying a cheap pair from a fast-fashion store, invest in a well-known brand that offers durable, high-quality boots. A higher upfront cost might feel like a stretch, but you won't need to replace them for several years.

Prioritize Meaningful Purchases

Think about the items and experiences that truly add value to your life. Instead of buying things you don't need or can do without, direct your spending to things that bring long-term happiness. For example, spending money on a vacation you've always dreamed of may be more fulfilling than buying the latest gadget that will soon be outdated.

- **Example**: Rather than buying the newest iPhone every year, consider taking a weekend getaway or investing in experiences that create memories. You'll have something tangible and fulfilling to look back on, rather than a phone that may only last a year or two.

Comparison Shop

Smart spending also involves taking the time to compare prices and find the best deals. Don't settle for the first price you see; do some research to ensure you're getting the best possible value for your money.

- **Example**: Before buying a large purchase, such as a new mattress or furniture, check multiple retailers and websites for the best deals. You may find the same item for a much lower price by simply taking the time to compare.

Look for Discounts

Use coupons, cashback offers, and sales to lower your costs. Many stores offer discounts for first-time customers, email sign-ups, or seasonal sales. If you're planning a big purchase, wait for the best time to buy. Black Friday and other holiday sales can provide great savings on high-ticket items.

- **Example**: Sign up for email newsletters from your favorite stores. Many offer a percentage off your first purchase. Additionally, check websites like RetailMeNot for coupon codes before making a purchase.

How to Get Started

Now that you understand the concept of smart spending, here are actionable steps to put it into practice:

1. **Track Your Spending**: Use budgeting tools or apps like Mint, YNAB (You Need a Budget), or PocketGuard to track your income and expenses. This will help you identify areas where you can cut back.

2. **Create a Budget**: Once you know where your money is going, create a budget that allocates a specific amount to each category—housing, food, entertainment, savings, etc. Stick to this budget as closely as possible.

3. **Identify Areas to Cut**: Look at your non-essential expenses and determine where you can make cuts. For example, you could reduce the number of times you eat out, cancel subscription services you don't use, or shop more strategically.

4. **Prioritize Savings**: One of the key elements of smart spending is making sure you're putting money toward your savings or investment goals. Automate transfers to your savings account or investment accounts so that you're consistently building your wealth, even when money is tight.

5. **Reevaluate Regularly**: Your needs and goals may change over time, so it's important to periodically reevaluate your spending and budget. This will ensure that you're always making the best choices for your current situation.

Example of Smart Spending in Action

Let's say you're able to identify $200 in savings each month by cutting back on dining out and subscriptions. That $200 can then be automatically transferred to an investment account or used to pay off high-interest debt. Over time, the money you've saved through smart spending can compound, creating financial growth without you having to sacrifice the things you enjoy.

Smart spending is about making intentional choices that support your long-term financial goals without making you feel deprived. By prioritizing your essential expenses, focusing on value rather than quantity, and being mindful of where you spend, you can significantly cut costs while maintaining a high quality of life. Implementing these strategies won't just help you save money—it will put you on the path to building wealth, even if you're starting with a modest income.

In the next section, we'll dive into finding free or low-cost joys that can enrich your life without straining your budget. Whether it's spending time outdoors, rediscovering hobbies, or enjoying simple pleasures, you'll learn how to make the most out of what's available to you without spending a fortune.

Finding Free or Low-Cost Joys

One of the most powerful ways to cut costs without sacrificing happiness is to find joy in activities that don't require spending a lot of money—or any money at all. It's easy to think that happiness comes from things you buy or expensive experiences, but often, the most fulfilling joys are free or low-cost. These activities not only save you money but also help you appreciate the simple pleasures in life.

Rediscovering Hobbies

Many of us have hobbies that we used to love but have let slide due to busy schedules or the pressures of life. The good news is that most hobbies don't require a significant investment of money to enjoy, and some may even be completely free. Rediscovering these hobbies can be a great way to bring joy and fulfillment into your life without spending much.

Examples:

- **Reading**: Libraries are a goldmine for free entertainment. You can borrow books, audiobooks, and even movies. Many public libraries also offer free digital downloads, including e-books and online courses. If you love reading but don't want to spend money on books, your local library is the best place to start.

- **Crafting**: Whether it's knitting, drawing, or DIY home decor, crafting can be an inexpensive way to pass the time and create something meaningful. You can often find free or low-cost supplies around your home. For example, old magazines can be turned into collages, and leftover fabric scraps can be used for sewing small items. There are countless online tutorials that show you how to make beautiful crafts with minimal resources.

- **Photography**: You don't need an expensive camera to enjoy photography. Start by using your smartphone to explore photography and experiment with angles, lighting, and composition. Many websites and social media platforms offer free photo challenges that can help you develop your skills while keeping the cost down.

How to Get Started:

- Check your local library for free books and activities.
- Join online crafting or photography communities to get tips and find inspiration.
- Use platforms like Pinterest or YouTube to learn how to start a new hobby with minimal investment.

Spending Time in Nature

Spending time outdoors is one of the easiest and most enjoyable ways to reconnect with life's simple pleasures, and it's almost always free. Whether you're hiking in the woods, visiting a park, or simply sitting outside and enjoying the fresh air, nature offers a multitude of benefits without a cost.

Examples:

- **Hiking**: Many areas have public parks or nature reserves where you can hike, walk, or simply sit and enjoy the surroundings. Research free or low-cost trails in your area. This is a great way to get exercise and unwind without spending money.

- **Picnics**: A picnic in a local park can be a relaxing and low-cost way to enjoy a meal outdoors with friends or family. Pack simple food from home or take leftovers to enjoy in the fresh air.

- **Stargazing**: If you live in a location with minimal light pollution, stargazing can be a magical, free experience. Simply find a quiet, dark spot and look up at the night sky. You can also use free stargazing apps to learn more about constellations and planets.

How to Get Started:

- Research free local parks and nature reserves near you.

- Plan a simple picnic with items you already have in your pantry.

- Find stargazing apps like SkyView or Star Walk to help you explore the night sky.

Free or Low-Cost Community Events

Many communities offer free or low-cost events, which can be a fun and social way to enjoy your surroundings. From free concerts to local festivals and farmer's markets, there are plenty of opportunities to engage in fun activities without having to spend money. These events can also be a great way to meet new people and explore your community.

Examples:

- **Free Concerts or Outdoor Movies**: Many cities and towns offer free outdoor concerts or movie screenings during the summer months. Check local community centers, city websites, or social media for schedules. Bring a blanket and enjoy the event with friends or family.

- **Farmers' Markets**: Visiting a local farmer's market can be a fun way to spend a Saturday morning. Not only can you enjoy browsing the fresh produce, many markets also have homemade goods and local crafts. Many markets also offer live music or free activities for children. The wife and I LOVE going to the local farmer's market, which just happens to be near a winery – another way to spend some time together (usually for just the cost of a bottle of wine to support our local friends and neighbors).

- **Volunteer Opportunities**: Volunteering is a great way to meet people and give back to your community without spending money. Many organizations rely on volunteers to help with events, food drives, and charity work. The time you spend helping others can bring a sense of fulfillment and joy.

How to Get Started:

- Check local event listings for free concerts, movie nights, and other community activities.

- Look for local farmers' markets or other outdoor events in your area.

- Research volunteer opportunities at local shelters, community organizations, or non-profits.

Socializing Without Spending Much

Spending time with friends and family is often associated with expensive outings, but socializing doesn't have to mean going out for drinks or dining at pricey restaurants. With a little creativity, you can have fun and strengthen your relationships without breaking the bank. Here are some ideas that the wife and I use ourselves:

- **Game Nights**: Host a game night with friends or family. Board games, card games, or even online games can provide hours of entertainment at little to no cost. If you already own the games, the only cost is the snacks and "beverages" you provide.

- **Potluck Dinners**: Rather than going out to eat, invite friends or family to a potluck dinner where everyone brings a dish to share. This way, everyone contributes, and the cost of food is divided among the group. We do this in our own neighborhood. We roll out the grills and coolers and enjoy each other's company. We also rotate hosts so that no one family does all the work.

- **DIY Spa Days**: Instead of booking expensive spa appointments, host a DIY spa day at home. Use inexpensive items like face masks, nail polish, and essential oils to create a relaxing atmosphere. You can also do this with friends or family to make it even more fun. This is one of the most fun days my wife and her friends have together. Sometimes, they even throw in some scrapbooking time, too.

Enjoying the Arts for Free

Culture and the arts can be enjoyed without spending a lot of money. Museums, art galleries, and live performances often offer free entry or discounted days, making them accessible even on a budget. If you live in a large city, many cultural events or performances may be offered for free.

Examples:

- **Museums and Art Galleries**: Many museums and galleries offer free entry on certain days or have permanent free exhibits. Even if there's an admission fee, it may be relatively low, especially compared to other forms of entertainment.

- **Street Performances and Festivals**: If you live in an area with a vibrant arts scene, there may be street performers, open mics, or local festivals that are free to attend. These events can provide hours of entertainment and allow you to experience different cultures and talents.

- **Theater Performances**: Many local theaters offer low-cost tickets or community theater productions. Check local listings for affordable shows or events in your area.

How to Get Started:

- Look for free or discounted museum days or events in your area.

- Attend local street festivals or performances.

- Research affordable or free community theater performances.

Finding free or low-cost joys is about reconnecting with the simple pleasures that are often overlooked in the pursuit of material things. By rediscovering hobbies, spending time in nature, attending free community events, socializing without spending, and enjoying the arts on a budget, you can create a life filled with fulfillment without constantly reaching for your wallet. In the next section, we will explore the importance of sustainability and long-term frugality, focusing on how to build habits that not only help you save money now but also create lasting wealth in the future.

Sustainability and Long-Term Frugality

Adopting sustainable and long-term frugality isn't just about cutting costs today; it's about creating habits that help you live within your means, invest wisely, and build a foundation for future wealth. Sustainable frugality is about making choices that prioritize value over temporary pleasure. This doesn't mean living without enjoyment or constantly depriving yourself, but rather adopting a mindset that focuses on long-term benefits and creating lasting financial security.

Long-term frugality doesn't happen overnight, but it's built through small, consistent habits that, over time, add up to significant savings and wealth. By choosing wisely today, you set yourself up for financial stability in the future. Here's how you can start.

Mindful Purchasing Decisions

Being mindful of what you purchase is one of the cornerstones of long-term frugality. It's easy to be tempted by flash sales, impulse buys, or the latest trends, but making purchases based on necessity rather than impulse can save you a lot of money. Mindful purchasing means being thoughtful about your needs, understanding the true cost of an item, and making purchases that align with your long-term financial goals.

Examples:

- **Avoid Impulse Purchases**: Create a shopping list and stick to it. If you see something that isn't on the list, resist the urge to buy it right away. Instead, wait 24 hours and see if you still feel the same way. This will help you avoid buying things you don't truly need.

- **Do Your Research**: Before purchasing a big-ticket item, spend time researching different options and prices. Often, there are multiple alternatives to the same product that can offer similar benefits at a lower cost. Look for quality products that will last, even if they cost slightly more upfront, as they can save you money in the long run.

- **Buy Secondhand**: Consider buying secondhand or gently used items. Websites like eBay, Facebook Marketplace, and local thrift stores can be great places to find affordable items, from clothes to furniture to electronics. Many high-quality items are sold secondhand at a fraction of the price, and some may even be in like-new condition.

How to Get Started:

- Start by tracking your spending to see where you can cut out unnecessary purchases.
- Research the long-term costs of items you're thinking of buying, such as warranties, maintenance, or upgrades.
- Check out thrift stores and online resale marketplaces before buying new.

Cutting Monthly Expenses Without Sacrificing Quality of Life

Many people assume that the only way to save money is to dramatically cut their lifestyle—switching to a smaller home, giving up vacations, or eating only ramen. But cutting back doesn't mean depriving yourself. Instead, look for small ways to reduce recurring costs without sacrificing your happiness or well-being.

Examples:

- **Reevaluate Subscriptions**: Take a look at all the subscriptions you're paying for each month—streaming services, magazine subscriptions, gym memberships, or subscription boxes. Many of these services have become so common that we don't even notice them anymore. Cancel subscriptions that you don't use or no longer find value in. You may be surprised by how much you can save by cutting back on these regular expenses.
- **Negotiate Bills**: For many regular bills, such as insurance, internet, or phone plans, companies are of-

ten willing to negotiate for better rates to keep your business. If you haven't done so recently, take the time to call your service providers and ask about discounts or promotions. If they won't offer you a better rate, consider switching to a competitor.

- **Cook More at Home**: Eating out or ordering takeout is convenient, but it can add up quickly. Instead, learn to prepare simple meals at home. Cooking in bulk can also help you save money by making multiple meals at once. Consider meal prepping on the weekends so you can save both time and money throughout the week.

How to Get Started:

- List all your subscriptions and evaluate which ones you use regularly and which ones you can cancel.
- Call your service providers to negotiate your bills, or shop around for better rates.
- Start meal planning for the week to reduce the temptation to eat out.

Investing in Quality Over Quantity

One of the key tenets of long-term frugality is investing in quality rather than quantity. This applies to everything from clothes to electronics to household items. While quality items may cost more upfront, they can save you money over time by lasting longer and performing better.

Examples:

- **Clothing**: Instead of buying multiple cheap items that wear out quickly, focus on buying fewer, higher-quality pieces. Look for clothes made from durable materials like wool, leather, or cotton, which will last longer than cheaper synthetics. A high-quality coat or pair of shoes might cost more initially but can serve you well for years.

- **Electronics**: When it comes to electronics, consider buying higher-end products that come with longer warranties and higher reliability. While a budget phone or laptop might seem like a good deal, it might need to be replaced in a few years, while a more expensive model could last much longer.

- **Furniture**: Like clothing, furniture made from durable materials will last longer and require fewer replacements. Opt for pieces made from solid wood or metal instead of particle board, which can wear out quickly. Even with higher-quality furniture, you can often find great deals by purchasing secondhand.

How to Get Started:

- Identify items in your home that may need replacing and research quality options that will last longer.

- Look for reviews and ratings on items before purchasing to ensure they're well-built and durable.

- Start investing in fewer, higher-quality pieces of clothing, electronics, and furniture.

Developing a Long-Term Financial Plan

Let's go over Long-term planning again. Yes, it's that important! Sustainable frugality isn't just about making small adjustments in your spending habits—it's also about having a long-term financial plan that helps you save and invest wisely. Start by setting financial goals and creating a budget that will help you achieve them. The more intentional you are about your finances, the easier it will be to stay on track and make progress over time.

Examples:

- **Create a Budget**: Track your income and expenses to develop a budget that helps you allocate money for savings and investments. Using tools like Mint, YNAB (You Need A Budget), or even a simple spreadsheet can help you keep track of where your money is going each month.

- **Set Financial Goals**: Outline both short-term and long-term financial goals. Short-term goals might include building an emergency fund or paying off credit card debt, while long-term goals could involve saving for retirement or buying a home. By clearly defining these goals, you can create a roadmap for achieving them.

- **Automate Savings**: One of the easiest ways to save money is to set up automatic transfers into a savings account or retirement fund. This ensures that you're consistently putting money away without having to think about it. Even small contributions can add up over time, helping you build wealth steadily.

How to Get Started:

- Use budgeting apps to track your spending and set savings goals.
- Identify your top financial goals and create a plan for reaching them.
- Set up automatic transfers to savings and investment accounts to build wealth over time.

Cultivating a Mindset of Patience and Consistency

One of the keys to long-term frugality is developing patience. Sustainable frugality is not about quick fixes or instant gratification. It's about making steady progress toward your goals, knowing that small changes today can result in significant benefits in the future.

Examples:

- **Focus on Long-Term Goals**: Avoid falling into the trap of "keeping up with the Joneses." It's easy to feel the pressure to buy the latest gadgets or take expensive vacations, but staying focused on your long-term financial goals will help you avoid unnecessary spending.
- **Track Your Progress**: Keep an eye on how much you've saved or invested over time. Tracking your progress can help you stay motivated and see how small, consistent actions add up to big results.
- **Be Patient with Investments**: Investing is a long-term endeavor. Whether you're putting money

into the stock market or saving for retirement, remember that results take time. Be patient and avoid making emotional decisions based on short-term market fluctuations.

How to Get Started:

- Set clear long-term financial goals and avoid distractions that could derail your progress.
- Track your savings and investments over time to see how far you've come.
- Stay patient with your investments, and remember that consistency is key.

Sustainability and long-term frugality aren't about depriving yourself—they're about creating financial habits that will serve you well for years to come. By making mindful purchasing decisions, cutting monthly expenses without sacrificing happiness, investing in quality over quantity, and developing a long-term financial plan, you can ensure that your frugality supports your financial goals. In the next section, we'll explore how to find balance between frugality and enjoying life's pleasures while also securing your future.

Conclusion

Cutting costs doesn't have to feel like deprivation. With smart spending, an appreciation for simple pleasures, and a long-term approach to frugality, you can live a rich and fulfilling life without sacrificing happiness. By focusing on what truly matters to you, whether it's experiences, relationships, or sustainable habits, you can cut costs effectively and build wealth over time.

Living below your means becomes a lot easier when you learn to appreciate the simple pleasures that cost little or nothing. A home-cooked meal, a walk outside, a good conversation, or even knocking out a goal you set for yourself—these things add depth to your life without adding debt. When you stop chasing status symbols or trying to keep up with other people's lifestyles, you find that what really fulfills you is usually far more accessible than you think. That shift in mindset is the heart of long-term financial wellness. Frugality isn't about being cheap; it's about being intentional.

As you reach the end of this book, remember that building wealth without a six-figure salary is not only possible—it's practical. It's done every day by people who stay consistent, focused, and thoughtful with their choices. The strategies we've covered aren't based on luck or shortcuts. They're built on discipline, patience, and clarity of purpose. If you take anything with you from this journey, let it be this: the quality of your financial life will always be shaped more by your habits than your income. Now, let's close this out by pulling all the lessons together and reminding you exactly why your future is worth the work. We will sum it all up in the final chapter.

Chapter 10: Wrapping it all Up

Throughout this book, we've explored how to build wealth on a modest income, emphasizing strategic spending, investing, and disciplined financial habits. Now, as we reach the conclusion, it's time to consolidate those lessons and develop a sustainable plan for lifelong financial security.

1. The Power of Consistency

Wealth-building is not a one-time event but a continuous process. The most successful individuals—whether they started with little or were born into privilege—achieved financial independence by maintaining consistency over decades. It's not about making one great investment but about repeatedly making smart financial choices.

Key Actions:

- Commit to regularly investing in your future through retirement accounts, brokerage accounts, and personal development.
- Automate savings and investments so they become second nature rather than an occasional decision.
- Set clear financial milestones (e.g., saving your first $10,000, reaching a net worth of $100,000, achieving financial independence).

2. The Importance of Adaptability

Financial markets, job industries, and personal circumstances change. What works today might not work five years from now. The ability to pivot and adapt is essential for long-term wealth-building.

Key Actions:

- Stay informed on market trends and economic shifts.
- Continue learning about new investment opportunities, side hustles, and wealth-building strategies.
- Diversify income sources to protect against financial downturns.

3. Avoiding Financial Complacency

One of the biggest dangers in wealth-building is reaching a level of comfort and then stopping financial growth efforts. Many people start strong but eventually plateau because they feel secure enough. However, wealth needs to be actively maintained and grown.

Key Actions:

- Regularly review your budget and investment strategy to ensure they align with long-term goals.
- Challenge yourself to increase savings and improve income streams even when financially comfortable.
- Keep lifestyle inflation in check—earn more but don't automatically spend more.

4. Teaching Financial Literacy to Others

A true sign of mastering wealth is the ability to teach it to others. By sharing financial knowledge, you reinforce your own understanding while helping others avoid common mistakes. That, indeed, is the entire point of this book!

Key Actions:

- Encourage financial discussions within your family and community.
- Mentor someone who is just beginning their financial journey.
- Teach children the value of money, saving, and investing early in life.

5. Preparing for the Unexpected

Even with the best financial plans, life happens. Medical emergencies, job losses, or market crashes can disrupt financial stability. Those who prepare in advance can navigate challenges with minimal disruption.

Key Actions:

- Maintain an emergency fund that covers 6-12 months of expenses.
- Have proper insurance coverage (health, disability, life, and home insurance).
- Keep debt low to avoid financial vulnerability during crises.

6. The Final Checklist – Are You on the Right Track?

To ensure you're on the right path to financial independence, ask yourself the following questions:

- Have I set clear financial goals for the next 5, 10, and 20 years? Remember *start* small but *plan* big!
- Am I consistently saving and investing at least 20% of my income? Obviously, you may not be here right now. That's okay, start small and build from broke.
- Do I have a diversified income strategy that includes investments, side hustles, and potential passive income sources? This very book is proof you can do it!
- Do I have a strong emergency fund and a plan to protect my assets? Don't forget this very important step.

Conclusion

Building wealth on a modest income is not only possible but achievable. The strategies outlined in this book are not quick-fix solutions, but proven methods used by financially successful individuals – including me. I also built from broke. Whether you're starting from zero or refining your financial approach, the principles remain the same: earn wisely, spend strategically, use the free tools available to you - such as AI and YouTube, invest consistently, and protect your future. You know where you're starting, and you know where you're heading. Keep moving, keep improving, and claim the financial independence you've been working toward. Don't let critics, review bombers, or unsupportive friends, family, or co-workers get in your way. The next move is yours. **Are you ready to take it?**

www.ingramcontent.com/pod-product-compliance
Lightning Source LLC
LaVergne TN
LVHW022107200926
848481LV00003B/1080